Within & Beyond
The Connection Revisited

Gayle Redfern

WITHIN & BEYOND
Copyright © 2020 **Gayle Redfern**

All rights reserved. No part of this book may be used or reproduced by any means, graphic, electronic, or mechanical, including photocopying, recording, taping or by information storage and retrieval system without the written permission of the author except in the case of brief quotations embodied in critical articles and reviews.

Stratton Press Publishing,
831 N Tatnall Street Suite M #188,
Wilmington, DE 19801
www.stratton-press.com
1-888-323-7009

Because of the dynamic nature of the Internet, any web addresses or links contained in this book may have changed since publication and may no longer be valid. The views expressed in the work are solely those of the author and do not necessarily reflect the views of the publisher, and the publisher hereby disclaims any responsibility for them.

ISBN (Paperback): 978-1-64345-460-3
ISBN (Ebook): 978-1-64345-851-9

Printed in the United States of America

Acknowledgments

This book could not have been completed without the support and guidance of my friends and professional experts, whom I now also consider friends. I want to thank each one for their encouragement and assistance.

    Marilyn Dyke for her artwork

    Marian and Henrika Pudek, she for sharing her channeled information and him for his photography.

    Dr. Linnea Battel of the STO:LO First Nations people who clarified the writing about the Xá: ytem stones and shared legends from her people.

    Finally, I thank my husband Bill for the hours he spent proofreading the manuscript and being my sounding board. I have often heard comments about how people couldn't accomplish something without their spouses. I now know why. It is almost impossible.

    My thanks and love to all.

Introduction

*"Somewhere, something incredible
is waiting to be known."*
Carl Sagan

"Wonderful how completely everything in wild nature fits into us, as if truly part and parent of us. The sun shines not on us but in us. The rivers flow not past but through us, thrilling tingling vibrating every fiber and cell of the substance of our bodies, making them glide and sing. The trees wave and the flowers bloom in our bodies as well as our souls, and every bird song, wind song, and tremendous storm song of the rocks in the heart of the mountains is our song, our very own, singing our love."

—John Muir

I'm reminded of a book I read several years ago. I loved the title and thought about how true and appropriate it is for many aspects of our life and learning. Bob Frissell wrote:

> **"Nothing in This Book is True,
> But It's Exactly How Things are."**

I would like to change this to read –

> **"Everything in This Book is True and It's
> Exactly How Things have always Been."**

What we have is a powerful relationship waiting to welcome into the fold.

Several centuries ago, around the end of the fourteenth century, Europe was hit with the bubonic plague. Normally, once you caught the disease, you died. However, some contracted it and did not die; others did not get it at all. This anomaly was the beginning of many superstitions and fears. It was not until the twentieth century that an answer was found. Scientists discovered the variance could be traced directly to the DHA coding. People who carried particular genetic pattern were protected.

This book is not about the physical attributes of humans. I learned that just as the genetic coding protected some people in the Middle Ages, today the Cosmic Life Pattern (CLP) protects some people from various ailments and opens up specific sources of more information.

As you move through this book, therefore, you need to remember that not everyone receives messages from rocks or sacred trees, crystal skulls or crop circles. We all receive information; the source just won't be the same as that of your neighbors.

Unlike many other books, this book was not written in order from beginning to end. Instead, it started with incoming information that fit in the middle of the book. For more than two years, there was no apparent pattern. It jumped from section to section with no apparent order. Most of this time, this simply confused and puzzled me, but then I realized this was nothing more than an example of *no such thing as time.*

I was able to set my confusion aside and let the information flow, knowing order would evolve. It was a reminder that order of any kind implies past, present, and future time, which is one of the three precepts in this book.

As you move through the book, you will see these concepts intertwined. They are Planes of Reference, Time versus No- time and Pleiadian energy.

Planes of Reference

There have been many adaptations or interpretations of the term *dimensions*. One of these definitions relates to the chakras and aura of the body. While it is not a popular definition, it exists nevertheless. Many people studied and worked with them believing there were higher chakras and lower chakras.

In this school of thinking, lower chakras must be balanced and cleared first before moving on to balance the higher chakras. However, both systems chakras and auras co-exist in the same space and are NOT separate. They are heard, seen, and felt as one. Sensitive people see the auras pulsating in a wave-like manner; the colors of the wave pull the energy of individual chakras. The chakras and the corresponding colors are:

1. Root-Red
2. Hara-Orange
3. Solar Plexus – Yellow
4. Heart – Green
5. Throat – Blue
6. 3rd Eye – Indigo
7. Crown – Violet
8. Transpersonal – Transparent or Clear

Another definition comes from the renowned author and lecturer, Barbara Hand Clow. Most of the information in her book, *The Pleiadian Agenda* was channeled from the Pleiadians. As I read Clow's book, I realized that her dimension definitions related in some way to the universe, suggesting to me that evolution or expansion is dependent upon the attributes accredited to the individual planets or groupings. Her definitions are:

1. Iron and Crystal Core
2. Telluric Ley Lines and Vortices
3. Linear Space and Time
4. Archetypes: Anunnaki
5. Love and Creativity: Pleiades
6. Morphic Fields Sacred Geometry: Sirius

7. Galactic Information Highway: Andromeda
8. Cosmic Order: Orion
9. Milky Way: Tzolk\in

Numbers five through nine are directly linked to stars and solar systems. We have individual planets – Niburu and Sirius; open clusters – Pleiades; constellations – Orion; galaxies – Andromeda and finally the Milky Way.

It is important to understand and accept the fact that *all* explanations are accurate whether they are historically known, unknown or just being discovered. Let us remember there is no such thing as time. Each description has a definitive purpose implying separation and distinctiveness. Suddenly the word "dimension" has a limited scope. It is time for humanity to look at the topic differently.

As I look back at the labels or layers, I realize they are another tool whose use was limited. Leaders in their quest for power, taught us to block most of this information and focus instead on the planes where they would, or they could, gain control.

What is rapidly becoming apparent is the fact that *everyone has simultaneous access to ALL nine planes of reference and has had this access since before birth.* Using our Planes of Reference -- or dimensions -- we can view or interpret any piece of information nine different ways. The planes do nothing more than focus our attention on a portion of our reality or what is seen.

The planes exist in a large full circle with nine sections, no beginning and no end. Looking at the complete circle from above, it is white. When we zoom in, we see that each section is a different color, much like the aura or chakra colors. If we shift our attention to a particular section of the circle, the overall color changes slightly, taking on a specific hue.

A good analogy might be a full symphony orchestra. When the entire orchestra is playing, we hear, and see, a beautiful work of art –a full circle. When a particular section, such as the strings is highlighted, there is still the full circle creating beauty; it just takes on a different hue. Superimposing the orchestra image onto our circle, the string section is made bold.

Another way of looking at the circle is looking at the traditional activities of an individual. A person can drive a car, sing a song, follow directions and perform simple mathematics all at the same time. When they need to read road signs, he or she may stop singing and pay more attention on the driving. However, her circle is still complete. Her attributes are still present and in constant use. All she has done is bring one to the forefront, shifting the hue of the circle slightly. We still have access to all planes but we have thickened the circle at one particular point.

I see the "Planes of Reference" or sections of the circle as:

1. The *solidity* key – tangible solid physical world or existence
2. The *texture* key – air and matter blends forming textures. This is the awareness of solid matter, the movement of energy and the relationship of all life.
3. The *identity* key – awareness of being in the physical body on the earth, including a survival protectiveness of self and others.
4. The *emotional* key – discovering and feeling the emotions of yourself.
5. The *empathy* key – compassion and sharing with others.

6. The *insight* key – expanding your potentiality, awareness of psychic wisdom.
7. The *spiritual* key – connected to all other energies.
8. The *guidance* key – knowing there is universal guidance without interference.
9. The *council key* – the ultimate connection.

Time versus No-time

"*There is no such thing as time. We are always in the present moment.*" Although this is becoming an understood and popular concept, it is still confusing to many people. To hear the statement that we are also living in the Dark Ages or the time of the Roman Empire sets some on their heels. However, if we pause for a moment, adjust our perspective, and look at the scenes from an alternate viewpoint, then it becomes possible. Here is an analogy to ponder.

Each one of us is but a small fragment of energy in the universe, almost like a fleck of dust. We contain everything that a larger piece holds, just a microscopic version.

Next, consider this fleck of dust being dispersed over a vast area. This scattering has been proven in today's scientific world.

The next step is to consider your brother / sister falling on the sidewalk not far from where you are standing. Today, people generally run immediately to their aid, looking for a safe solution.

Now if this brother or sister is in a scene that occurred several hundred years ago, we cannot physically help them. However, we *can* send healing and loving energy as compassion. We need to remember they did not ask to be in that time but they are there nevertheless. We have the tools so why not share them.

We won't change history, but we can modify it.

The purpose of this analogy is to remind you that all people on all planes in all times have all the tools they need. We simple need to know how to draw upon them. Usually all we need to do is ask and trust.

As people evolved, there was a need to understand events and to understand how we looked at those events. We looked for a description of what happened. One useful explanation was the term *dimensions,* because it implies movement between different realities or bodies. We needed something that supported our concept of past, present and future, so we used the term **time**.

At this point in our evolution though, metaphysical authorities are reminding us there is no such thing as time; everything is NOW. Therefore, "Planes of Reference" becomes a more appropriate title than *dimensions* as it does not imply a physical progression. Since it does not have a built-in reference to the passage of time, it gently reminds that there is no such thing as time.

As you continue reading this book, you will discover yourself. You will realize at first that switching from plane to plane is slow and cumbersome, but soon you are doing it quickly and unconsciously. The information has always been around us, but until we accepted the principle that there was no time and the planes of reference were within us; it could not be seen. This is how it was, and is, for the majority of people. For a small population though, it has always been available because they were cognizant of planes and not dimensions.

It is fascinating to observe these two groups slowly blending into one. Fortunately, more people than ever before trust the information they receive and work with this expanded repertoire of knowledge.

In spite of this evolution in thinking, there is still a need to write as though time does exist. The human mind is logical and frequently reluctant to let go of old habits. It is easier to stay in the linear world than to have everything swirling around us. However, to be able to understand fully, we need to know how to switch from plane to plane.

These are key points for us.

- The signs may have evolved from what was long ago, but to understand them, understand that they are communication in the NOW.
- The Sacred Trees carry information valid in any time period. It isn't understood unless we view them in the NOW.
- To understand the Crystal Skulls and the Earth Designs, we need to be balanced and accessing ALL planes.

Finally, to help understand all of the above, we need to understand the MANU NYMBA and the related crystalline clusters. This is the core resource of bringing your being into balance.

Discovering these wonders turns out to be one of the wonders of life, almost like learning to read for the first time. The principle of time versus no-time is *within* all of us taking us *beyond* the normal realm of reality.

Pleiadian Energy

Introducing and exposing people to the Pleiades and their loving, peaceful nature is not new. Although this open cluster was mentioned as long ago as 1000 BCE, it has been a myth essentially throughout history. Astronomers, theologians, and sky watchers identified the Pleiades as a star cluster in our Milky Way galaxy.

While there is no tangible evidence, we also know there is an energy entity known as the Pleiadians who have had a long and loving interest in our planet. Generally their policy is to observe only, no interference. However, when they feel it is in the best interest of the Universe to assist, they do so.

Several thousand years ago, they intervened in the lands of Lemuria and Atlantis. To a lesser degree, we see their involvement with the Australian Aborigines. They tried assisting other cultures, but unfortunately they were not always successful. Still, they tried but on a much smaller scale, placing energy seeds in all cultures at different points of evolution.

In this way, they were able to work quietly with beings on the Earth planet, gradually exposing small groups or individuals to more "Planes of Reference." They knew there would always be beings that could benefit from knowledge and wisdom, so they left deposits of information and the necessary access tools. A study of indigenous people of various countries supports this.

There are always Wise Ones on the Planet.

Pleiadian energy surrounds every particle of energy in the universe – within our planet, over the entire surface and throughout the cosmos. Some may refer to the energy differently, but my choice is *Pleiadian.*

This energy teaches us to access the "Planes of Reference" simultaneously. Their influence is a major part of our evolution. The no-time knowledge flowing through for this book states where the Pleiadians could intensify their involvement.

The time had come for us to become aware of their existence, a full circle

Contemplating this, you may identify several other sources of similar information. You may also ask: *If this information has been around since the origin of the planet, why couldn't we see or interpret it?* There are two answers.

The first is that knowledge is for the greatest good of all. Most energy beings, including the Pleiades want the information for peace and balance, not power. Unfortunately we have a history in which there were always humans who were only too willing to interpret the information for others as a way to gain control and feed their own egos. The result was a society of people living on Earth who experienced fear and imbalance.

The second answer is that it is important to remember that when information comes from the universe, it does not come to only one person or in one form. Instead, the data flows forth down many paths, allowing recipients to follow the path of their choice. It is also possible that you existed in a region of fear or on a plane where the information was blocked. This is one of the joys of working with universal knowledge. With so many sources, individuals discover the wisdom in their own way in their own time.

This book introduces us to the MANU NYMBA, the *Nucleus of Life* that exists in all living entities throughout the universe. It is here that the internal imbalance is felt the most. Although we have known about the components individually (geometric structure, crystalline energy) for some time, their relationship was unknown. The core design may be universal but for us to exist in harmony in the universe, each isolated core design must be independently balanced.

Unfortunately, the Pleiades have had to sit and watch in silence as we learned the hard way. They saw us struggle with power, greed, imbalance and learning. Gradually though, we intuitively began balancing our inner being. This gives us a balanced MANU NYMBA and increased Pleiadian influence; giving a well-earned and viable trust.

The result is a plethora of information available in such a variety of styles that every human on this planet now has access to all portions of universal wisdom. The Pleiadian guides are helping us balance our MANU NYMBA and discover new knowledge. There is now a choice for the individual, for by using whatever "Plane of Reference" they want, people can receive information through a channeled message, wisdom stored in sacred tree, a crystal skull, or perhaps an earth design. This can be looked at as being *in transition*. We are learning and discovering. Consequently, it is important that we become receptive to new information and discover our personal method of leaning.

People still have different requirements. Fortunately, the Pleiadian guides recognize this and supply information in various forms. They selected writers for automatic writing to produce books with the necessary verbatim text. Two other examples are Barbara Marciniak and Barbara Hand Clow. These authors share the love and wisdom of the Pleiades.

In addition, our guides from beyond the earth plane assured that the crystal skulls were appropriately placed and more Earth Designs were drawn where they would be discovered at appropriate times. Once individuals decide to trust their feelings of true and good, the information from whatever source becomes powerful.

One of the prerequisites for discovering skulls, earth designs and other data repositories is having your personal MANU NYMBA in balance. While it is possible to explore and discover the wonders of the world without a balanced MANU

NYMBA, the understanding of the messages will be extremely limited. Therefore, we begin with the **MANU NYMBA** section before moving on to other connected wonders.

THE MANU NYMBA

*"The beginning of knowledge is the discovery
of something we do not understand"*
Frank Herbert

Knowledge of the Star Tetrahedron, or the **MER-KA-BA**, has been around for quite some time, certainly since Socrates and Plato introduced sacred geometry to the world. In the beginning, sacred geometry was not spoken of as such, for fear of death. Those in powerful positions considered it counter to their religious beliefs.

Pythagoras, the earliest of great Greek philosophers and mathematicians, recognized the importance of these shapes and also how they represented the elements of alchemy. However he did not allow the subject to be discussed outside his school. Socrates, 469- 399 BC understood the spiritual connection of geometric shapes. He too did not speak openly of this. By the time Plato became a student of Socrates, around 300 BC, he was able to speak of it, but only with trusted friends.

I mention this brief history not only to emphasize just how long this knowledge has been with us but also to provide a reminder of who understood the importance in the past. These philosophers recognized that each geometric shape represented one of the elements necessary for life, not only on this Planet but through the Universe. Their discovery was advanced and relevant in their time but the human race has now moved far beyond their basic philosophical use of geometric shapes.

Today, in the 21st century, understanding the meaning of the MER- KA-BA opens a new world of thinking to the reader. It is no longer simply a shape used by mathematicians; but is recognized as a vehicle surrounding our bodies. Once we learned how it functioned, we were able to travel freely between dimensions. This is ancient knowledge.

There is also something very similar, but not readily recognized. It is the **MANU NYMBA.**

It is the same shape, a star tetrahedron. However, unlike the MER- KA-BA which surrounds the body, this star tetrahedron is *within* the body and is the smallest microscopic particle of life, smaller than the atom. It is this minute particle, the MANU NYMBA, from which all life and light evolves. It contains the Akashic records, DNA of the Universe and all information that is readily accessible to every life form in the cosmos. It can be described as the Cosmic Life Pattern (CLP).

The MER-KA-BA and the MANU NYMBA -Distinctions

The analytical mind will discover that MANU NYMBA can be defined many ways and each word is found in many languages. Some will ask: If there is a similarity between the internal and external star tetrahedrons, then why not give them the same name? Through channeled information, I was told that the internal star tetrahedron MUST be called MANU NYMBA. The two tetrahedrons may be similar but their differences are great.

The MER-KA-BA assigns male and female energy to each of the star tetrahedrons while the MANU NYMBA assigns magnetic and electronic energy.

The MER-KA-BA is for traveling between dimensions. It is assumed to surround a physical entity but this is not always the case. A MER- KA-BA can exist in the universe simply as a small particle of energy that floats between the dimensions. It is when this particle, the MER-KA-BA, slows down and gives up the synergy of movement that the MANU NYMBA is allowed to be born.

What causes the MER-KA-BA to slow down, I do not know. Understanding the physics and other physical sciences is far beyond my knowledge and the scope of this book. Nevertheless, we do need to understand that both the MER-KA-BA and the MANU NYMBA carry the memory of the universe and all living energies of its creation.

The MER-KA-BA stores the memory but it is not utilized while the star tetrahedron is in motion. It has to slow almost to a standstill, begin growing the crystal cluster and THEN the memory is activated. The strength of the MANU shifts from moving between dimensions to balancing and growing. We need to understand the relationship and similarity but it is more important for our learning to think of them as two entirely different and separate parts of our being.

Both are powerful, both needed for life and neither should be ignored.

MER-KA-BA is made up of three words believed to have come from ancient Egypt. In Hebrew MER-KA-VAH means chariot.

MER refers to *two counter rotating fields of light spinning* in the same space or place *ascending.*

KA refers to the *individual spirit, or the light body;* also defined as *Movement of the Light body*, the spark of light being the smallest component of the source life itself. The light body that surrounds us is lighter than the air on this Earth Plane and therefore is able to flow through the air, into other physical entities, traveling throughout the Universe. Some also call it PRANA, Life Force or CHI.

BA is the *physical reality*. When there is no physical form, then VAH is the concepts or interpretation of the reality that they (the spirits) bring with them. Looking at the **BA** then, the *spinning counter rotating light* becomes the vehicle that takes our spirit and body from one world or dimension into another.

Place ascending not only refers to where we are going and also the direction. All energy is reduced to a small particle of light, spinning faster and in a smaller space than the atom.

If you are looking for a more rational explanation, the smallest particle is *ascending* into larger form.

The two words, MANU NYMBA, are ancient and while the original meanings are lost, we still have the power behind these words. Many people decry the lack of written history, forgetting that spoken history carries the power of a meaning far easier than the written word.

Depending upon the spelling, MANU NYMBA origins can be traced through Polynesian, Sanskrit, Tibetan and various languages of Africa. It is truly universal. The definitions vary somewhat but there are also similarities.

The Polynesian definition of **MANU** means *invisible, all pervasive energy found in the air, imponderable,* and necessary for all beings[1]. It is the Vital Life Force, the quality of motion of the essence that brings everything to life.

There are several different uses of **NYMBA** but the meaning we use is *the connection to all other life beings on our planet and elsewhere in the Universe.* Through this connection, we carry our DNA, Cosmic Life Pattern (CLP) and Akashic memories.

The Greek mathematician, Pythagoras, introduced the Star Tetrahedron as part of Sacred Geometry approximately twenty-five hundred years ago. Thoth, the Ascended Master, introduced the MER-KA-BA approximately five thousand years ago. Today one of the most popular sources of Thoth's wisdom comes through the mediumship of Drunvalo Melchizedek. This wisdom refers to the MER-KA-BA being a vehicle for moving through realities. In addition, Melchizedek talks about it creating our own reality. As an isolated, singular spirit or soul, we *are* a total being of body, mind and spirit or *Light of our Spirit.* [2]

The emphasis of these teachings is learning how to move between realities or dimensions, believed to be necessary for our soul's growth. There are many methods showing ways to do this; more than adequate if this is all you want to achieve. This concept can be limiting. There is so much more to living and learning than simply moving between dimensions. Today, we have the opportunity to look at ALL the information available to us. Once we have this knowledge, THEN, moving between dimensions takes on a new meaning.

---

[1] Bletzer, June G. PhD, *The Donning International Encyclopedia Psychic Dictionary,* Whitford Press, West Chester, Penn., 1986

[2] Melchchizedek, Drunvalo, *The Ancient Secret of the Flower of Life, Vol. I,* Light Technology Publishing, Flagstaff AZ, 1998, p5 ff.

One purpose of the MANU NYMBA is to store information. It contains ALL knowledge from all our lives, all knowledge of the entire Universe, DNA of the Universe, wisdom from the planet and all information that is readily accessible to every life form in the cosmos. It becomes true wisdom and unconditional love.

The Hindu refers to this as the Akashic Records. The Kabbalah from the Hebrew refer to it as the text containing the sacred, secret structure of the Universe. We have access to so much more knowledge. As more of our DNA strands are activated, even more information is there for us to see and use.

The key vital knowledge here is:

> The MER-KA-BA is the same for each person. The MANU NYMBA is *different* for each person.

At this point, we need to ask ourselves just what is *our* reality?

How does our reality differ from others? We are all given the same information and yet we see it so differently. How does our reality give us access and yet we come away with diverse interpretations? When we look at this, then we may understand what is meant by *Light of our Spirit within the body or reality.*

While the NYMBA contains Universal information, it also contains the DNA records. This Universal information is standard but how we look at it depends upon when and where we were born. Astrological charts illustrate this for each human being. We also need to look at the axis of the Earth plane and the relationship to the planets closest to us. Later we will talk about the information given to us through each planet. However, for now, we need only to understand that over time, as the Earth's axis shifted, it placed planets in a different position. This altered the information coming to us from each planet.

The Universal knowledge, then, will differ slightly according to where and when a person lives. Conversely, the DNA records vary greatly since each person has their own personal stamp of DNA code. This gives an individual the information of the physical past through their family.

In addition to these two variables, we also have the lessons and information gathered by the soul through many lives. This may contain the universal knowledge but each life a soul lives alters the emphasis.

Let me give examples of these last two variables. The DNA code carried by a farmer in Africa in the 20th century will be different than the DNA carried by a scientist born into the same century. If we moved both into the 21st Century, they would be different yet again. They may be a little closer in similarities but still limited because the knowledge and experience of each affects the DNA strands.

You may think that two brothers in the same family would carry the same DNA. However, what if one of the brothers/souls has lived only 20 lives on Earth, while their brother's soul has come to Earth more than 200 times. The experience memory would be very different. We must remember that even though the physical brain may not remember other lives, our soul does.

It is important that we accept these variables and remember them as we go through this book. It is these differences that give each individual his or her own reality. Therefore, no two people will see something in the same way. Even in the same family the perception or reality is different for each one, depending upon placement in sibling rank, age of soul or exposure to events. We also need to remember that each person born into this world comes with their own purpose or goal in life. It is this purpose, experience and DNA records that determine how each sees life and reality.

These differences are what make each human an individual. We are living according to the information *we have available to us,* creating our own personal reality. This ensures that each individual is right. Consequently, if everyone is right, then there is no wrong and therefore then each human being must be perfect. Accepting that each one of us is perfect, we can then freely accept another's outlook and send universal love to the entire world without fear.

Scope and Reality

If this is true, then the scope of each MANU NYMBA is perfect and is our own reality. As a result, not only are we separate, unique and special but so is our MANU NYMBA. No two are alike. Difficulty understanding or accepting any portion of this book is perhaps because you have a different reality and what is not understood is not pertinent to you as an individual at this time. One person may need to relate to only the MER-KA-BA description while another needs to include the MANU NYMBA. It is not simply that one person pays more attention to detail than another; it is simply that each of us will use the MER-KA-BA and MANU NYMBA knowledge differently.

How we absorb the information will help us achieve the goals and plans that we are meant to complete at that time.

To clarify this further, imagine yourself standing on a small point of land. What do you see? Do you see the vast, calm ocean in front of you? Or do you smell the breeze and see the ragged rocks covered with barnacles and sea weed immediately below where you are standing?

Both visions are part of the reality of life. If you look only at the distant oceans, you may lose your footing and fall if you step off the point of land. This, however, shows us the vastness of the Universe and emphasizes the smallness of our being. Staring only at the ragged rocks stops you from embracing the calmness or receiving the warning of the imminent storm. Nevertheless, these rocks remind us of how small life forms can be and just how interdependent they are. It is like seeing many small galaxies in one place separate, yet interconnected.

The traditional description of the **MER-KA-BA** defines it three ways.

The **MER**, the counter-rotating lights, do not only rotate around a single entity. The bands of light intercept and mix with the lights of all other entities. Similarly, the **KA** -- PRANA or CHI -- are not isolated within or around a single entity. It flows within one, around one and connects with another. The **BA** is the physical reality of each small entity and the physical reality of the cosmos.

The MER-KA-BA then, is an *external* Star Tetrahedron surrounding our body and connecting our external bodies with everything around us.

Many cultures have myths and recorded history older than Western civilizations that speak of energy coming from the Earth and the Sky. For them, this energy is both opposing and unifying.

For example, in China, the MER-KA-BA and MANU NYMBA became the TAO. YIN is the magnetic energy tetrahedron flowing from the Mother Earth. YANG flows from the Sun bringing electrical energy. They show the TAO as containing energies that are both independent and yet dependent upon each other. Similarly, native cultures understand the importance of directional energy of North, South, East, West, above and below. This is the same for our Star Tetrahedrons. Both have energy flowing from Earth and Sky.

The MANU NYMBA refers to the star tetrahedrons *within* our body carrying either magnetic or electrical energy.

This powerful **MANU NYMBA** carries all knowledge, keeping us centered and in perfect harmony with everything around us. The MANU NYMBA's balance is dependent upon the fluid surrounding it. If for any reason, the host body becomes dehydrated or the purity of the fluid is altered, the balance is severely affected. Our bodies need this fluid for three functions.

One is the balance of the *individual* MANU NYMBA.

Second is the balance of the complex *chain* of MANU NYMBA. Third is the birth and growth of each *crystal cluster.*

This is clarified further on, but it is important to remember that the MANU NYMBA refers to individual, chains and clusters, all important connection of life and the foundation of all living beings. Humanity is just beginning to discover the wondrous complexity of life.

Both vehicles, MER-KA-BA and MANU NYMBA are STAR TETRAHEDRON shapes.

A Tetrahedron is a four sided polyhedron. Looking at it on paper, you only see two-dimensions but in reality, it is a three dimensional figure with all sides being equal. The Star forms when two tetrahedrons are overlapped with one point directed to the Earth (receiving the magnetic energy) and another directed to the Sky (receiving the electrical energy). To help clarify it for the reader, the points are marked so the viewer can identify the electrical tetrahedron as points A, G, E and F. The Magnetic has the points B.C.D. M and G.

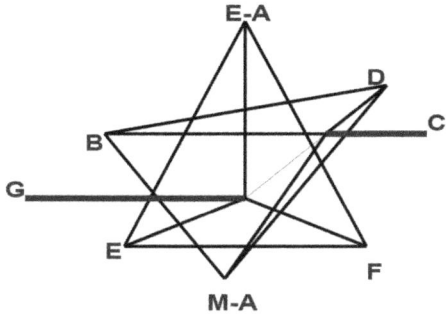

Information coming from the spirit side comes in a form familiar to the individual such that it can be readily understood.

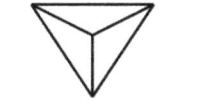

Earth or Magnetic Tetrahedron

Imagine separating the Star Tetrahedron in front of you with one of the tips pointing to the Earth (called the Earth tetrahedron). This point brings up the *magnetic* energy up from the Earth.

Sky or Electrical Tetrahedron

Then, turn the Star Tetrahedron one quarter turn so that the tetrahedron facing you has one point facing into to the sky (called the Sun tetrahedron). This point is drawing the *electrical* energy from the Universe.

When we imagine that we are standing ABOVE the Sun tetrahedron, this is what we discover.

1. The energy flow combines the Earth and Universal energy into one central, supercharged core, strengthening the entire flow. This core is where the magnetic and electrical tetrahedron joins.
2. When you look at the total Star Tetrahedron, it appears to be moving from left to right. This is because the magnetic, energy flows clockwise and the electrical, energy flows counterclockwise.
3. A balanced MANU NYMBA moves at a high velocity, which is what produces this illusion of movement. This rotation sends all the important information such as cell memory and universal knowledge throughout the entire being.
4. When one of the tetrahedrons goes out of balance, it tips the other, minimizing movement or flow of information. This is when illness or disaster can strike. A person can develop any illness depending where the imbalance originates, stomach, brain or heart area for example.

Society and Balance

This link applies not only to individual living beings but also to groups such as a single society. We tend not to think of societies or social groupings as a living entity but they are very much alive, just more complex. An excellent example might be Atlantis and Lemuria.

Atlantis, a segment beneath the Atlantic was known for mathematical and scientific developments – logical left brain studies. The tetrahedron coming from the Earth carries the magnetic energy, grounding and functional in nature – left brain.

Lemuria, beneath India and Pacific Oceans, was known for the intuitive, creative strengths – emotional or right brain functions. The tetrahedron coming from the Sun, or Sky carries the electrical or intuitive attributes.

The left brain energy was grounding and functional in nature. The right brain functions were intuitive and creative. When the connection of these two went out of balance, both societies fell ill. There was no recourse if societies refuse to take healing action.

The extent of balance goes far beyond one specific component of our world. It is important to remember that what we do WITHIN our body affects BEYOND our system and what happens BEYOND our body affects it WITHIN.

Here in the modern world, we are just beginning to understand that individual health, society and the Earth itself all affect one another, some in a greater degree. Other cultures have known this for some time. Ayurveda medicine from India, native healing from indigenous nations and oriental Medicine (TCM) from China all recognize the importance of this connection between the Earth and humans.

Ayurveda medicine incorporates the times of year and day into their healing. TCM speaks of the elements of the Earth as well introducing us to the meridian system of our body. Half of the channels bring up the energy from the Earth – YIN. The other half bring the energy from the Sun – YANG.

This cross-cultural comparison brings out two essential points.

Cultures much older than our Western society knew the importance of the interrelation between what went on outside our body and inside our body.

It doesn't matter what health system or scientific research you study, all the information can be reduced to a single MANU NYMBA. Ancient healing methods may not specifically define the attributes of the MANU NYMBA but the many aspects WERE corrected.

We need a constant reminder that the MANU NYMBA is the very core of our existence, the true CLP.

It is smaller than an atom, self-sufficient, yet dependent upon the surrounding life. It is the smallest element within our body, carrying the universal wisdom. As it grows, the cell expands, sharing knowledge and sends love and healing. Without the CLP, there is no existence of the Life Force.

The drawings in this figure give us a single MANU NYMBA how the cells connect around an isolated MANU NYMBA. This allows a small MANU NYMBA to *within* a cell or connecting many cells carrying all records of life, including DNA of the body. Here, the MANU NYMBA is necessary to program the cell that is the germ of creation.

#3: Many cells, one MANA NYMBA

#2: The MANA NYMBA

#1: Sngle cell & One MANA NYMBA

The top one labeled -- #3 -- shows the smallest component of the body with a very small MANU NYMBA *inside the circle or* cell carrying all records of life, including DNA of the body.

The next one, labeled -- #2 -- shows the MANU NYMBA without the circle reminding us that this is the Akashic records or the Hebrew text of sacred, secret structure of the Universe. How can a living being be created if it did not contain all the information necessary?

This MANU NYMBA continues in many sizes at all levels of our being, within the cell, within the body. It carries all pertinent knowledge, connecting the cells as well as linking with other energies in the Universe, sharing knowledge and sending love and healing. In our hypothetical single cell has propagated by splitting into many cells, carrying the information into each new cell. As the new cell is formed, a new MANU NYMBA is also formed, carrying all the necessary information. It then forms a larger with the new attached cells.

At times it can be difficult to see the MANU NYMBA at so many stages and levels. When we remember that this pervasive energy is our connection to all forms of life in the Universe, it becomes easier to see it on multiple levels. It carries our identity into the cosmos, allowing us to join and share. It is life itself. Life vibrates with the energy. It is the vibration that allows us to send information or heal.

Personal awareness comes through in the best sensory way. The two most used are sound and sight.

The Sound of the MANU NYMBA

Drunvalo Melchizedek correlated the musical notes with the MER- KA-BA. This also fits our **MANU NYMBA** since they are both star tetrahedron shapes.

Drunvalo details the musical system extremely well in his ***The Ancient Secret of the Flower of Life*** publications. Musical notes, provide us information on the vibrational speed for each point. It also provides us with the *toning* notes for healing and balancing. Initially, we will follow his system as it provides a very clear system. Then we can apply our additional information to the system.

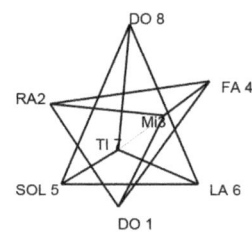

Figure 1
STAR Tetrahedron and the notes of the scale

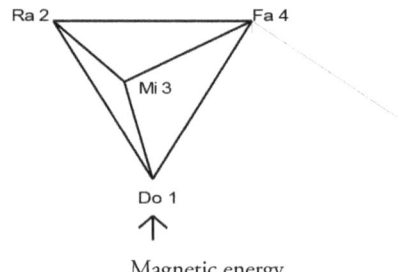

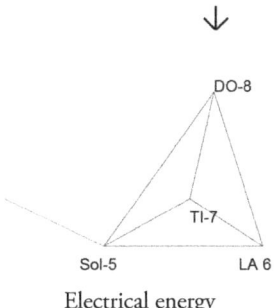

Electrical energy

In the top drawing, the energy enters the Star Tetrahedron from the Earth at the bottom of the magnetic tetrahedron, the note **Do**. Each Tetrahedron has four notes. The notes for this tetrahedron start at the bottom of the figure $Do_1 \rightarrow Ra_2 \rightarrow Mi_3 \rightarrow Fa_4$.

To the untrained eye, the energy carries on flowing up from the note next in line until it reaches the **Do** of the next octave: $Sol_5 \rightarrow La_6 \rightarrow Ti_7 \rightarrow Do_8$. You can see how they connect in this sample drawing.

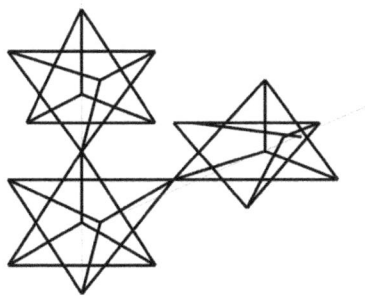

This drawing shows how the three MANU NYMBA come together. to form a chain. They are linked by a magnetic/electrical conduit that farriers the energy throughout our entire body. This conduit becomes VERY important when we talk about the balancing and connection to other life energies.

The common area between the two tetrahedrons is called the **SUPERCHARGED CORE.** This name comes about because it carries both electrical and magnetic energy. The flow of energy moves in two directions joining, or mixing, both energies at this location.

We get the magnetism from the Earth, flowing up into the Universe. Plus we get the electrical energy flows from above, following the same lines to enter the Earth at the base. The strength for the object occurs comes when two tetrahedrons overlap producing a supercharged core or the common area of both tetrahedrons.

If either tetrahedron is out of balance for any reason, then this supercharged core becomes misshapen, causing any number of difficulties.

Even though the drawing of the conduit above only shows a small segment of the CORE connection, visualize billions of MANU NYMBA inside a body. Then speculate on the complexity facing the viewer or scientist of the amazing web joining these two.

When we review the microscopic foundation, as the host cell grows and expands; imbalances might range from infant malformations, or illness throughout our lives.

While these illnesses or injuries manifested within the physical being, they can potentially carry the imbalance to other Star Tetrahedrons throughout the World or Universe.

Historically, most historic writers and teachers speak of only one pathway, or channel, through our body, the Chakra system. However, the one that aligns the MANU NYMBA is a tube running *parallel* to the Chakra line. It connects the Earth and Sky tetrahedrons transporting all pertinent information. I hear many voices objecting, stating that the Chakra system is the only way to pull CHI energy into our bodies. However, when we remember that we are speaking of minute tubes, then it becomes viable for the two to run parallel in such a small area that it is easy to assume that they are one.

This maze, or series, of hollow tubes is none other than the meridian system of our body. I prefer the label "meridian" over channel or vessel because of the definitions. The popular definition of meridian is a line or circle passing through the two poles (head and feet). This is exactly what is happening in our bodies. Each meridian is a tube running through the top and bottom of the STAR tetrahedron up to the head and down to the Earth, bringing in the magnetic and electrical energy that is so vital to our life force.

The main tube connecting the many MANU NYMBA within the body is called the *central and governing channels or vessels* by health practitioners. Without realizing the complexity of the information, the Chinese are accredited with identifying the meridian system for Traditional Chinese Medicine. The SUPERCHARGED CORE is the acupuncture or acupressure points of TCM.

LINKING OF MANU NYMBA

Going back to the musical theme, those who familiar with music know that the scales Do-Re, Mi, etc. can be placed anywhere on the musical scales. To begin playing any instrument, the player finds **C,** *middle* **C.** Is it not logical to look at the body the same way? If this is so, then the scale would start at **G**, regardless of whether you are moving from feet to head or head to feet. Middle C then sits in the Heart area of all Star tetrahedrons, midway in the energy flow, between the Mi and Sol. This is the SUPERCHARGED CORE where the magnetic and electrical energy converge; the region where emotion and loving energy is supercharged in a balanced body.

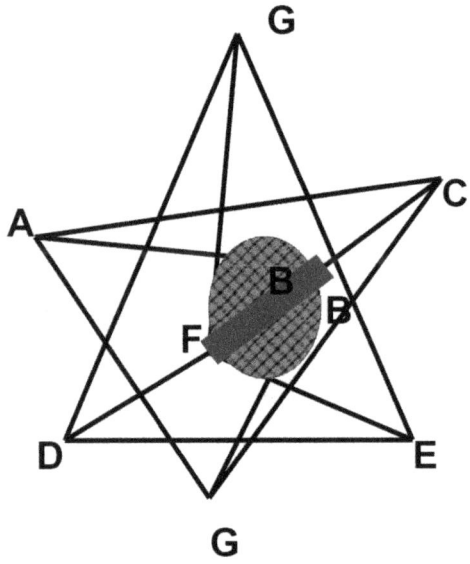

MANU NYMBA WITH NOTES OF SCALE OF G

As musicians, we understand that notes vibrate. Many people though forget that color also vibrates. It is the combination of these that become the two parts of our information that link beyond our single living being.

MANU NYMBA COLOR

Color is an important component of our entity and the Universe. It is the color vibration that allows the MANU NYMBA to move within, around and through the systems.

Middle C is **red,** known to be vitality, hot and stimulating. Is this not necessary for the emotion and universal love that is so necessary for balance? The note A at the base of the magnetic tetrahedron note at the base of the magnetic tetrahedron is **green**, providing a pure solid connection to the Earth below. Green is known for growth, new beginnings, balance and health.

When the MANU NYMBA is in balance, color flows evenly and smoothly from one area to the next. There is no need to specifically connect one color at one spot to one note. Just as in a rainbow, you see the individual colors but where they stop and start is indefinable. The colors of the magnetic tetrahedron flow from green to yellow to orange to red, showing an overall soft yellow glow.

This glow shows an aliveness coming from the Earth, generating growth from the previous MANU NYMBA just as it becomes a new, complete Star tetrahedron.

Vibrational movement is essential for the healthy inner functioning of any life form. It is relatively easy to visualize the movement, though it may appear in an unorthodox pattern. This is the order of the rainbow colors, which define movement.

The energy flows from middle C, through the supercharged Core to G. It then travels up to high A where it continues to flow in an *anti- clockwise direction.*

When you match notes to colors, you get the following order:

- Middle C — red
- G — indigo
- High A — green
- B — yellow
- E — orange
- Low A — green
- F — purple
- D — blue

From there the energy flows into the next MANU NYMBA. As the MANU NYMBA moves, it displays the colors in a soft, vibrant glow.

In the electrical tetrahedron, the colors flow from red to purple to indigo to blue producing an over blue glow when it is in balance. This hue is what many call a blue light and seek it in their spiritual path. Again, there is no specific delineation of color but the colors are there, flowing into each other as in a rainbow. We see the beauty of this in a balanced MANU NYMBA. Here, the reflection of the Orange and Red on the Blue gives it the green color, which is the Magnetic energy of the second MANU NYMBA.

When all the colors of two balanced tetrahedrons merge in the SUPERCHARGED CORE, they produce a pure, bright white. However, if the MANU NYMBA is out of balance, we see instead a shadow of the hue out of balance. This tells you what color or note is needed in your body to return the CORE to its pure white serenity.

The notes and colors continue their flow, moving from one MANU NYMBA to the next, along the chain of the double helix.

Double Helix

The main key for understanding this complexity is remembering that the MANU NYMBA is the smallest component of life, as we know it today. The MANU NYMBA contains all the universal information needed for life as well as establishing our identity as an individual.

This information is mandatory for the SEED of life, the TREE of Life, transportation, our DNA; in fact everything we do in the physical form originates here. Perhaps it also has the soul information but this cannot be proven. As the cells recreate or grow they also re-create the DNA for each cell.

Cell with DNA strand emerging from its center, followed by a drawing of an expanded strand, or strands, creating a **Double Helix**, the core of our DNA.

This image shows a double helix with 4 chemical strands, identified by scientist, called bases, making up a genome. This genome is nothing more than a set of instructions for each strand representing one for four chemicals or proteins.

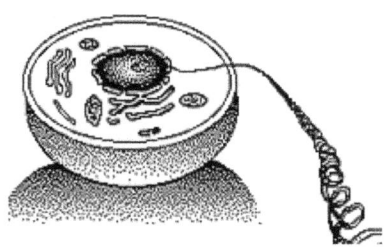

Cell with DNA strand emerging

Double Helix showing 4 chemicals

Each MANU NYMBA carries magnetic energy from the Earth and electrical from the Universe, connecting the two strands. If a single MANU NYMBA is out of balance, a chain reaction results.

First, the individual MANU NYMBA goes, then the two connecting the two strands go and then the DNA helix itself is put into an imbalanced state. Hence, we see one situation that show up as physical illness. To further complicate matters; if the fluid varies in any way, then the associated MANU NYMBA is affected.

The Universal link and the MANU NYMBA

Earlier, we stated that all universal knowledge is within each MANU NYMBA, duplicating it multiple times within our body. This includes a link with all planets within our solar system. There is also a possibility that these links expand to include all planets in the *Cosmos* but for now we will limit ourselves to our solar system. Although we have stated that the magnetic energy comes from the planet and NOT from the universe, this power overlaps and is absorbed from all sources universal and planetary.

The following figure and table clarifies this, showing the connection. This relational information provides tools that will be explained in the next section. There, we look further at the characteristics that each holds. It is these characteristics providing focus when we are trying to balance our MANU NYMBA.

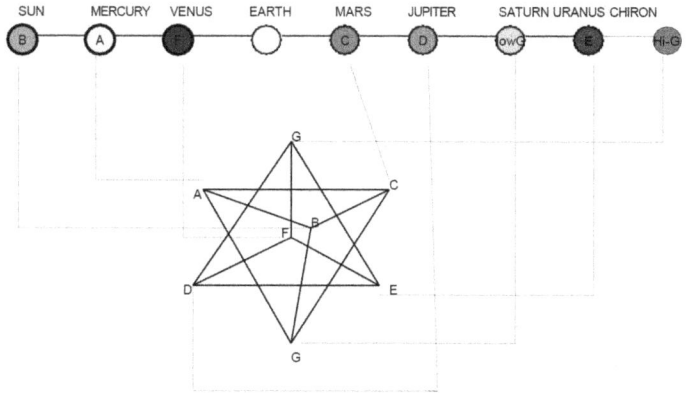

MANU NYMBA, THE PLANETS AND THE ASSOCIATED COLORS

The figure above shows us which tetrahedron each planet is connected to us, the color and main characteristic. The data in the table below gives the same data, just in a different format. The Earth, its Moon, Neptune and Pluto are not included above but because of the powerful influence on our well-being and balance, they are included in the table.

Musical Note	Specific Tetrahedron -- Magnet or Electrical	Planet	Color	Main characteristics
Low-G	Magnetic	Saturn	Green	Stability
A	Magnetic	Mercury	Yellow	Wisdom
B	Magnetic	Sun	Orange	Bravery
C	Magnetic	Mars	Red	Leadership
D	Electrical	Jupiter	Violet	Spiritual
E	Electrical	Uranus	Indigo	Dignity
F	Electrical	Venus	Blue	Love & Harmony
Hi-G	Electrical	Chiron	Blue-Green	Intuition
	Magnetic	Earth	White	Physical stamina
	Electrical	Moon	Gold	Overall healing
		Neptune	Blue & Red	Physical healing
		Pluto		Relaxation

PLANET ASSOCIATIONS, COLOR AND CHARACTERISTICS

The Planets

Mankind has known for eons the power of our connection to the entire Universe. The planets and moons that are closer to Earth have more impact upon us and therefore can be used for healing and balancing. In this book, we use 7 planets, one star (our Sun), our planet Earth and our single moon. Now we have a dilemma.

First, historically, we have visual images of many of the planets which include a color. Secondly, astronomy gives us a color.

Then, during a meditation, I was shown a different color again. Since we are using the color for a specific purpose, I am following the information coming from meditation. At this time, we are not concerned with size, rotation or composition, but they do impact the color choice and the individual characteristics.

Sun A main sequence star shines because of the massive, fairly steady output of energy from the fusion of hydrogen nuclei to form helium. In the Star Tetrahedron, the Sun is on one edge of our supercharged core. It gives us *energy* and *bravery*. The color *orange* compliments the note "B". The attributes and the colors are very strong. We need to be very aware of what is going on in our lives before calling upon the Sun's energy.

Mercury orbits closer to the sun than any other planet, making it dry, hot, and virtually airless. Although the planet's cratered surface resembles that of the moon, it is believed that the interior is actually similar to the earth's, consisting primarily of iron and other heavy elements. It is known for the *wisdom* that it can transmit to us. For balancing and healing, we look to Mercury for the wisdom brought to us from the Earth since it is in the Magnetic Tetrahedron.

Venus is the brightest object in our sky, after the sun and moon. It is *blue*, giving us *love and harmony*. It is also electrical, balancing the upper tetrahedron.

Earth provides an oxygen-rich and protective atmosphere; moderate temperatures, abundant water, and a varied chemical composition allow earth to support life, the only planet to do so. *White gives us physical stamina.* White is the most centering of all as it contains all colors from the rainbow as well as the universe. For this book, however, we have only listed the colors and traits from our galaxy.

Earth's Moon is one of the most influential of all the Universal masses. We need to acknowledge the Ebb and

Flow of the Energy. While it doesn't correlate with either Tetrahedron, we can call upon the energy according to the cycle. Pictures show dark seas, or maria, the two bright-rayed craters Tycho (near bottom) and Copernicus (directly north of Tycho). Because the moon is so close to the Earth, the effect is profound. Earlier, in **Inner Bridges**, the effect on our eating and planting patterns was given. For the MANU NYMBA, it is not specifically connected to the Star Tetrahedron but is *magnetic,* gold in color and has strong healing features.

Mars' thin atmosphere consists primarily of carbon dioxide, with small amounts of nitrogen, oxygen, water vapor, and other gases. For balancing, it is magnetic, *Red* in color and provides us with *leadership*. It is part of the supercharged core balancing.

Jupiter is the largest of the planets. The bands are caused by strong atmospheric currents and accentuated by a dense cloud cover. There are moons surrounding this planet. Four of these are: Europa, center, nearest Jupiter, Io upper left, Callisto lower left, and Ganymede lower right. Jupiter is *Violet*, giving us our *spiritual* balance. It is part of the electrical tetrahedron.

Saturn is distinguished by its rings, ranks as the second largest planet—Jupiter is the largest—in the solar system. It appears slightly mauve with a yellow/golden color. However, we need to look at the color as *green* for its connection to the Earth and she gives us *stability*. For healing and balancing, Saturn is magnetic and at the base of the Magnetic Tetrahedron.

Chiron has traditionally been classified as an asteroid. It orbits the Sun in an eccentric orbit, between Saturn and Uranus, which takes it close to both of those major planets. When we view through a telescope, we see that Chiron has a dark surface. It is a *blue-green* giving us a connection to our *intuitive* abilities. It is at the top of the electrical tetrahedron.

Uranus Photographs show a blue-green color that comes from the methane gas present in its cold, clear atmosphere. The electrical attribute balances the *indigo* color, which contributes to the dignity balance. Uranus is used to help balance the electrical tetrahedron when the bottom portion gets out of balance.

Neptune Many feel that pictures from the 1989 Voyager 2 mission gave a false image of Neptune. However, when you understand that Neptune gives us *physical healing*, then the *blue* and *red* make sense. When you focus on this planet, your understanding of numerology will increase.

Pluto is farthest from the sun than the other planets in the solar system. However it occasionally moves in closer than Neptune due to an irregular orbit. This planet gives each of us mental balancing, perhaps because it has an irregular orbit, it is capable of absorbing our imbalance into its orbit. Like Neptune, focusing on Pluto increases your understanding of numerology. Interestingly, Pluto does not give us specific properties as it is too far away for a strong influence. However, when we need to be *relaxed* and *playful*, Pluto energy helps. It carries a gentle loving energy.

BALANCING THE MANU NYMBA NETWORK

Applying this information to help our body and everything around is actually quite simple. There are several ways or methods which you can use to bring the body and MANU NYMBA into balance.

USING SOUND AND COLOR

Previously, we spoke of the strength and power of the vibrational energy within our body. We now know that the MANU NYMBA is this energy. Therefore, it is not surprising that the most effective way to balance the MANU NYMBA in our body would be to use the vibrational energy of sound and color. While this is most effective way, unfortunately, it can also be the most expensive and most structured.

Regardless, I recommend using this procedure whenever possible. Since it requires equipment, a structured environment plus the help of another person it is not practical to use for personal balancing.

For a complete balance, you want to start at the base of the Earth Tetrahedron, locate the *a low G and the color green* and move up through the two tetrahedrons; then taking a small step back to finish off balancing the Super-Charged Core.

Your objective is to move through the tones smoothly and evenly at the same time as the subject, or client, visualizes the even wave of the spectrum of colors flowing from one point to the next.

It is very important to always move **UP** the scale. Moving in the opposite direction can throw the person into even greater imbalance.

Preparation:

1. You will need a complete set of good quality **tuning forks**.
2. A clear uncluttered corner of a room or a **large screen** that arcs around the back of the person to reverberate the sound into the person. Since you will be in front

of the person approximately 5 feet, you want the tone to echo BACK from the screen or corner into all parts of their body.
3. Comfortable straight chair.

Procedure:

1. Have the person sit in the corner or in front of the screen, facing out with feet flat on the floor. You will stand approximately 5 feet in front of the person.
2. Line up all the tuning forks in an ordered row – Low-G, A, B, C, D, E, F, and High-G.
3. Explain that as you are "tuning" each fork, the person will switch over to the spectrum flow for the appropriate note. This flow through the notes would be
   a) Low-G: Green to yellow
   b) A: Yellow to orange
   c) B: Orange to Red
   d) C: Red to Violet
   e) D: Violet to Indigo
   f) E: Indigo to Blue
   g) F: Blue to Green
4. Have the subject close their eyes and 'see' the wave of the spectrum flowing from the first color to the second.
5. Until the person is completely familiar with the tones and colors, as you move through the tuning forks, inform the person which particular spectrum to visualize.

MEDITATION

There are three meditation techniques that can be used. The first two are for personal healing. The first is **silent,** the second uses a **mantra.** The third technique sends healing to a person or persons.

METHOD ONE– Silent Meditation:

STEP I – Going into the Meditation:

Go into a meditation using your favorite method. If you are unfamiliar with mediation, then I recommend the following:

- To help you focus, have your choice of soft, gentle music playing quietly.
- Sit upright in a comfortable chair with your hands in your lap, palms facing up and your feet solid on the ground, parallel to each other.
- Take three deep breaths, breathing slowly. Slowly count to 4 as you breathe in, hold for 4, and count to 4 as you slowly breathe out. Repeat this three times. On the third intake, hold your breath and ask the following questions.

STEP II – Asking questions:

These are suggested questions. Naturally you will intuitively lead to pertinent questions.

1. What characteristics do I need at this time to improve the balance of my MANU NYMBA and my crystal cluster?
2. If it is appropriate, please tell me what planet I need to connect with at this time.

3. Please tell me the color and/or musical note that I need at this time.

METHOD TWO – Using a Mantra

OPTION I – Meditating for personal balancing

1. Sit in the appropriate position for meditation. Take three breaths, using a count of 4 as outlined above.
2. On the third breath intake, ask for guidance in balancing your internal MANU NYMBA.
3. To bring balance into your body, slowly repeat the Mantra – **MY MANU NYMBA**, using a single syllable on each breath either going out or coming into your body. MY-MA-NA-MYM-BA.

Continue repeating this mantra as long as necessary. After a while you will be so deep that you are no longer aware of the words. Do not be concerned about whether you are doing it *right*. Your body knows.

NOTE: If you are tuned into your body, you will feel a gentle alignment happening in your body. It is a great feeling.

OPTION TWO -- Meditating to heal other life energies:

1. Sit in the appropriate position for meditation. Take three breaths, using a count of 4 as outlined above.
2. On the third breath intake, ask for guidance in balancing the MANU NYMBA belonging to another person or living entity. (Remember that societies are living entities!)

3. When you are repeating the Mantra, if the name of the entity is short, then use it. For instance, if you have a friend *Sally* who needs healing, then use – **SAL-LYS- MA-NA-NYM-BA.** Otherwise, simply state in Step two, who this mantra will be for and give the name. This is applicable for places with long names such as the United States. Regardless, use a single syllable on each breath either going out or coming into your body. MA-NA-MYM-BA.
4. Continue repeating this mantra as long as necessary.

ENERGY CONDUITS

We spoke earlier about the many methods of balancing and clearing the meridians, often called channels, in the body. Generally, the acupressure or acupuncture points are used. Science has proven that these points possess electrical conductivity[3].

These points work extremely well on clearing and balancing the electrical tetrahedron. Following this logic, we would have to assume that balancing the electrical tetrahedron would, simply through association, balance the magnetic tetrahedron. This assumption, though, is not always correct. For instance, if the crystal cluster is responsible for the imbalance, then you need to directly balance the magnetic tetrahedrons. It is also possible that you muscle-checked the person and verified the need for magnetic tetrahedron correction; discovering that the person is suffering from emotion stress or brain tension. For

---

[3] Zhu Zong-xiang. "Research advances in the Electrical Specificity of Meridians and Acupuncture Points." *American Journal of Acupuncture 9 no.3 (July/Sept 1981):203-215*

whatever reason, you may want a simple, direct, solution; a solution that works for balancing the entire MANU NYMBA Network.

When we demonstrated the linking of MANU NYMBA earlier, the intent was to show the reader the beginning of a complex network of conduits. What was not shown was that *all* the conduits are connected to two main channels in the body. This applies to wherever the network resides, be it the human body, societies or tribes of people or living entities in nature. These two conduits are called the central and governing conduits.

While both run from the lower part of the body up to the head, they still carry both magnetic and electrical energy since they are made up of MANY MANU NYMBA. The central conduit runs up the front from the pubic area to the *lower* lip. The governing conduit runs up the back from the base of the spine up and over the head to the *upp*er lip.

When the energy is blocked in either of these channels, it affects the *entire* system. We need to remember that they are connected to tubes taking the energy in and away from the Earth and the Sun.

There are two ways of unblocking these channels; both use the energy of our bodies or the universal energy such as Reiki energy.

1. The first way is to place the index and middle finger of your *left* hand at the entrance and place the index and middle finger of your *right* hand at the top of the meridian. Hold this position until you can feel a pulse at each end.
2. This way is often simpler. Hold your hand about 1 inch, 3 cm, away from the body. Starting at the base

of the invisible channel, slowly run your hand from the base UP the full length of the channel. Remove your hand completely from the body and repeat several times. The reason we take the hand away completely is that moving the hand in the opposite direction negates the clearing we have just completed.
3. Since it is difficult to run your hand up your back and over your head in one uninterrupted flow, if the governing channel is blocked, solicit help.

CRYSTAL ENERGY & THE MANU NYMBA

**Individual drawings of
MANU NYMBA & Crystal Cluster**

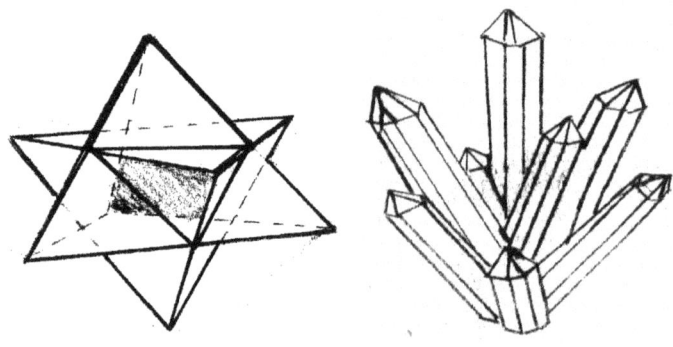

**Double Unit: MANU NYMBA
aligned with crystal cluster**

WITHIN & BEYOND: REVISITED

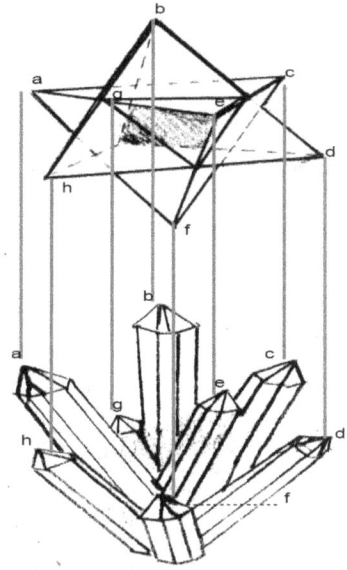

This section of the theory can be one of the most dynamic and illuminating pieces of knowledge. It provides a connection to much of our knowledge that has been buried (or lost).

For hundreds of years, since the time of René Descartes we have been taught to regard the organs of our bodies as separate pieces of equipment, each independent, each living on its own, not necessarily regarding the needs of other parts of our body. Other cultures knew differently and finally today, we are beginning to agree.

As our culture advances, we discover that all functions and good health can be reduced to the MANU NYMBA and the connected crystal clusters.

Above are two separate drawings, one of MANU NYMBA and the next of a crystal cluster.

Second is the double unit showing their connection. Perhaps you can visualize them either on top of one another or in a vertical line. To help see them in your mind's eye, imaginary lines are drawn between the two units connect the points of the Star Tetrahedron and the crystalline cluster, hence a double, interdependent unit. They are also labeled for convenience. The letters have no other significance, they are not musical notes.

The MANU NYMBA provides balance within the body and the connection beyond the body, the Earth and all other planets, the seed of our being.

However, it does not stand as the only seed.

Its seed partner, **crystalline cluster**, carries energy, power and the nutrient needs for the body. Together they share the growth and health of the body plus all characteristics enjoyed by the individual body. We cannot accept one without accepting the other.

Scientists have proven that crystals, when compressed produce electricity. This is called *piezoelectricity*. The article "Crystal properties" in the 2002 publication of Encarta Encyclopedia reads: *some crystals, when compressed, develop electrical charges at their ends; other crystals develop similar charges when heated.*

This shows the system on a grand scale. Within this grand scale, our body tissue, are billions of MANU NYMBA and their connective crystalline clusters. Since these two units are connected, there is a finite amount of pressure joining them. When the MANU NYMBA goes out of balance, the pressure on each cluster point is altered.

This pressure must be an *exact amount* to avoid unnecessary electrical charges or heat. If this does not happen, then the entire system is thrown out of balance. This can be seen as lack of oxygen, reduced nutrients, sore muscles, or strain on organs – all visible on the grand scale as illness. Our scientists may not see the MANU NYMBA or the crystalline cluster but they do see the outcome.

Billions of minute crystal clusters are responsible for the absorption of oxygen and the absorption of nutrients. If the MANU NYMBA is not balanced then uneven pressure occurs. The outcome might be one of various malfunctions. The crystalline clusters stops growing and stops absorbing. This also works in reverse. If there is not sufficient oxygen or nutrients, then the MANU NYMBA is thrown out of balance, inviting illness to step in.

To better understand the complexity, compare a grain of sand inside an oyster shell. Under the right conditions, it produces a pearl. At conception of life, under the right conditions, the MANU NYMBA grows and multiplies. When it is perfectly balanced and fed, then the crystalline clusters begin to grow; bringing in all that we need for life. Both are sources of love and knowledge for the individual. These two units interact closely.

The crystal cluster keeps the MANU NYMBA aligned. The MANU NYMBA supports the growth and function of the cluster. I have no idea if two pearls are ever produced in one oyster shell but our mythical oyster does produce two, each dependent upon the other.

One of the necessities for the growth beyond a single MANU NYMBA is the need for the surrounding fluid to be unpolluted as much as possible. With the right conditions, sufficient, uncontaminated fluid and a balanced Star Tetrahedron, then a crystalline cluster will also grow. The health and success of this production rests entirely upon the host body.

If the connection with the surrounding Earth and other planets is weak, then the balance of the MANU NYMBA is shifted. If there is not equal amounts of fluid around the entire MANU NYMBA or if there are not sufficient nutrients, then the cluster will not grow properly, if at all. These conditions affect *everything*, the MANU NYMBA, the cluster, the cell and ultimately the entire body.

We realize that good health for body, mind and spirit is important but so often we do not realize how early it must start and the severity of the repercussions. Almost all new parents make sure that there is sufficient fluid for the newborn but many are not concerned about the purity of it.

Today, whenever possible, babies get breast milk rather than formula. Mothers usually stay away from drugs and alcohol. It is not always apparent, though, that mothers and mothers-to-be should drink distilled water, avoid junk food, and whenever possible, eat organic food grown right in the area where they live.

The nutrients and the energy of the region are always transferred to the baby either through the umbilical cord or the breast milk. Thinking before eating or drinking helps put the baby on the right path to health and helps the new body to produce pure crystal clusters. These clusters can then absorb oxygen and draw the nutrients from the foods during the child's life. It is surprising how the body can respond to the training or programming it receives.

To clarify: The water content of our bodies makes up 98% of our body's composition or 98% H_2O. Quartz crystal composed of approximately 28% silica (SiO_2), is gradually created from this fluid. Scientists may argue that quartz formation requires extremely high temperatures. For our wondrous body, this is not the case, since the clusters are so minute that they can evolve without the extreme temperatures. The one delightful thing about our body is that the temperatures are relatively constant. It is this constancy that performs where there is no extreme heat.

In the free space around the MANU NYMBA there are many small cavities, filled with the fluids of the body. As the temperature changes, quartz crystal is formed.

In my first book, INNER BRIDGES, published in 2002, I emphasized the importance of eating and living according to the region where you live. One of the reasons is the effect on the body temperature. In a hot climate, the crystal is formed at a higher bodily temperature; in cold climates, cooler temperature. The standard temperature of our body is 98.6°F or 37 °C. However, it is the range that becomes important.

The accepted range is 36.4° - 37.2°C and 97.5° – 99°F. These ranges are not large but this is all that is needed to respond to the hot or cold climate conditions for the crystal within our body. In cold climate, the crystal grows at the lower temperature; in hot climate, it grows at the higher temperature. If you live in a cold climate and your body temperature is at the high end of the range, the crystal will not grow as fast, if at all. The same is true if you live in a hot climate.

In the high climate, the body needs to keep the temperature at the high end of the range. If this is done, then assuming all other factors are favorable, the clusters will grow, keeping the MANU NYMBA in balance.

The purer or healthier the fluid around the MANU NYMBA is, the purer the crystal becomes. Many skeptics will argue that it is not necessary for quartz crystals to be pure to be effective. If the use is for general purposes outside the body, then this is true. In fact, impurities may enhance the function.

However, our internal network requires purity. The purity of this crystal within the body depends upon many factors.

There are approximately 60 chemical elements used in our body. These are shown in the corresponding table below *Elemental composition of the Body.*

Should the ratio or amount of any single one element change in any way, the purity is affected. Today, this can be extremely difficult to correct, especially when we hear from scientific experts that we do not have the nutrients in our food that we had 50 years ago. Supplements are not always the answer as we do not have accurate, personal information regarding the status of our personal body.

A number of years ago, I used muscle testing in my health practice for identifying the needs of the body and not the desires of the mind. As example, a friend was very proud that she took all the supplements that she felt she needed. Each pill was a blend of vitamins and minerals. At her request, I muscle tested her to see if each pill was the right one for her body.

What these tests showed was that she needed **ONE** of the vitamins in a particular pill but her body had sufficient of the other ingredients. In other words, she was over-dosing her body with some of the vitamins, potentially harmful to the body. She now uses muscle checking on a regular basis to determine her requirements and then switched over to swallowing capsules where each one contained only one vitamin. It meant she had to take more pills but she was not endangering her life-long health.

There are excellent books available providing more details on muscle testing, or Applied Kinesiology, also known as Biokinesiology.

For an infant or young child, it is usually safe to assume that their MANU NYMBA is balanced and the crystals are clear. For them, using a tool such as muscle testing is not necessary. Muscle testing, however, is an excellent means to verify what is needed before readjusting your lifestyle. It is certainly less expensive and more practical than blood tests. The first and best place to start is ensuring that the minute crystal clusters in our body are pure and ready to receive all they can. On the following two pages is a listing of the composite requirements for a 70 kg body.

When you look at this listing you will notice that the amount needed of the trace elements is extremely small. This does not mean that they are unimportant; four examples below the listings show us this.

Elemental composition of the Body[4]

Element	Mass of element	Element	Mass of element
oxygen	43 kg	chromium	14 mg
carbon	16 kg	manganese	12 mg
hydrogen	7 kg	arsenic	7 mg
nitrogen	1.8 kg	lithium	7 mg
calcium	1.0 kg	cesium	6 mg
phosphorus	780 g	mercury	6 mg
potassium	140 g	geranium	5 mg
sulfur	140 g	molybdenum	5 mg
sodium	100 g	cobalt	3 mg
chlorine	95 g	antimony	2 mg
magnesium	19 g	silver	2 mg

---

[4] Emsley, John, *The Elements*, 3rd ed., Clarendon Press, Oxford, 1998, from the Web: http://www.neosoft.com/~uthman/elements_of_body.htlml

iron	4.2 g	niobium	1.5 mg
fluorine	2.6 g	zirconium	1 mg
zinc	2.3 g	lanthanum	0.8 mg
silicon	1.0 g	gallium	0.7 mg
rubidium	0.68 g	tellurium	0.7 mg
strontium	0.32 g	yttrium	0.6 mg
omine	0.26 g	bismuth	0.5 mg
lead	0.12 g	thallium	0.5 mg
copper	72 mg	indium	0.4 mg
aluminum	60 mg	gold	0.2 mg
cadmium	50 mg	scandium	0.2 mg
cerium	40 mg	tantalum	0.2 mg
barium	22 mg	vanadium	0.11 mg
iodine	20 mg	thorium	0.1 mg
tin	20 mg	uranium	0.1 mg
titanium	20 mg	samarium	50 μg
boron	18 mg	beryllium	36 μg
nickel	15 mg	tungsten	20 μg
selenium	15 mg		

Rubidium is the most abundant element in the body (0.68 g) that has no known biological role. **Silicon**, which is slightly more abundant, may or may not have a metabolic function. However, we have learned that silica, or silicon dioxide, is necessary for blood, muscle, nerves, skin, nails and hair. **Vanadium** is the body's least abundant element (0.11 mg) that has a known biologic role, followed by **Cobalt** (3 mg), the latter being a constituent of vitamin B_{12}. Vitamin and mineral supplements may not even have them. Therefore we need to look for an alternative way to get them.

The body's 43 kilograms of **oxygen** is found mostly as a component of water, which makes up 70% of total body weight. Oxygen is also an integral component of all proteins, nucleic acids (DNA and RNA), carbohydrates, and fats.

The result of keeping the MANU NYMBA balanced and the crystalline clusters pure is the additional oxygen that is released to our body. When the system is in balance and synchronized, we get more oxygen and are able to take nutrients out of our food more efficiently. There are products on the market today designed to increase the oxygen in our bodies. Some do work very effectively but as stated, supplements are not always the best answer. Each reader must look at both the region where they live and their lifestyle. If they are living in a polluted city or in an area that has been stripped of its soil nutrients and/or the lifestyle is not optimum, THEN supplements may be necessary.

There are three simple steps to keep the crystalline clusters pure and growing at an optimum level.

1. Keeping the MANU NYMBA balanced using some of the methods listed earlier.
2. Ensuring that the majority of your food source is organic and grown in our home region. For more details on this subject, I refer the reader to my first book, **INNER BRIDGES.**
3. The third step is taking a teaspoon of organic, pure cranberry juice every morning in northern regions or a teaspoon of pure papaya juice in tropical climates. Prior to 5 years of age, this is not necessary as the balance and purity should come from food sources.

Regrettably, because there are missing elements in the soil and food, we end up with an incorrect blend of elements in our system. This causes imbalance, pressure on the crystal points, and slows growth. All these affect the MANU NYMBA and the body itself. If we can counteract this imbalance, then the crystalline clusters stays pure and balanced; everything works perfectly plus the amount of oxygen absorbed into our cells and bloodstream increases. We then get the maximum nutrients available necessary for our body's health. This maximum may not completely meet the body's needs. Unfortunately, with the changing environment, this may be all that is available. Having balanced, pure crystal clusters helps the system decide what is needed and what is not. We can then get the most available.

Impurities tend to remain with the clusters so it is imperative to start before birth working toward the optimum goal. Even though they remain in the crystals, this is not to say that because we are now grown and didn't know any better; that we have to live with what we have. Not so. We may have the clusters already formed, but what we do with our bodies today and in the future influences the growth and intake of nutrients.

For example, pollution plugs the intake of oxygen and nutrients into the crystal. Once the crystal is plugged, these undesirable chemicals overflow into our bloodstream and the rest of our body. Iron, carbon monoxide are two examples. We must remember that since these clusters regulate the amount of fluids and water in the body, if pollutants have plugged our systems then won't be able to manage the fluids in our bodies correctly.

The natural course of logic tells us that once we become adults, we don't have to worry about crystalline growth. Again, this is not so. These minute clusters are always growing and changing. There is an infinitesimal core of crystal carrying the impurities forward but we can keep this to a minimum.

Avoiding future impurities not only helps reduce the effect on both the clarity but also the rate of growth.

Peterson in Science News, April 22, 2000 reported a study on crystal growth rates that was completed in association with The Gale Group and Look-Smart in Farmington Hills, Michigan. He discovered that the amount of impurities affects the rate of growth of crystals. We must remember that the crystalline clusters formed under pressure and for them to grow it must be the *exact* amount of pressure. When the growth is altered, then the balance of the MANU NYMBA is altered. This then throws the entire body out.

Balancing and sending love to other humans and societies

So far, our personal MANU NYMBA and Crystal Clusters have been our only concern. Once we understand our internal balance and growth, then we can optimize our help given to others. The degree of our clarity decides how much help we can send to others.

Before becoming too downhearted, there is a solution. Healing can be sent as a group effort, maximizing the effectiveness. Also, the group does not have to be in one location, there simply has to be what can be known as *an agreement of plans*.

The <u>first</u> step is to decide who or what needs to be healed or balanced. Having a picture present may help.

The <u>second</u> step is to identify what quality is out of balance; this tells you the point or tetrahedron that needs attention.

The <u>third</u> step is looking at chart of planets, notes and colors to find out what tools to use. You may want to place a picture of the planet in the circle, use the color or possibly a

MANTRA. As we have said, there are many ways to center the MANU NYMBA and the cluster.

The <u>fourth</u> step is deciding upon a time and place and putting your thoughts into action.

Some people doubt the effectiveness of distant group thought. In 2001, shortly after the New York disaster, Art Bell during his nightly program called upon all listeners, asking them to concentrate on a single, positive thought at a specific time. The results were quite amazing.

As part of the research conducted under the name **Global Consciousness Project**, Bell conducted a random number generator experiment. These details are found on Art Bell's Web site -- http://artbell.com/gcp.html which is copied, with permission, from Art Bell's site.

Graph of Results from Thursday's Experiment,
October 2001 Provided by Dean Radin.

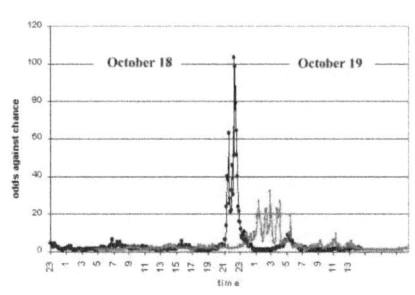

Times are in Pacific Time.

Random Number Generator Experiment

An obscure result of understanding and applying this knowledge is the effect on the CLP. The CLP for all on the earth plane and, I'm sure, through the universe, will benefit. One of the more subtle benefits of this practice is that as we gradually balance our MANU NYMBAs and grow pure crystal clusters, we will be using both the oxygen and the general nutrients on our planet more efficiently. IF we are using these more efficiently, then there will be more for all living species PLUS our health system need to do is look back over time and observe how society has adapted to a changing lifestyle.

Since the MER-KA-BA is for traveling between dimensions, it is assumed to surround a physical entity. However, this is not always the case.

A MER-KA-BA can exist apart in the universe simply as a small particle of energy that 'float's between the dimensions. It is only when this particle slows down and gives ups the synergy of movement that the MANU NYMBA is born.

Both the MER-KA-BA and the MANU NYMBA carry the memory of the universe and all living within. It is only then the MANU NYMBA slows to almost a standstill and begins to grow the crystal cluster that the memory is activated.

THE SACRED TREE, THE GIFT FROM LEMURIA

> *"If you foolishly ignore beauty, you'll soon find yourself without it. Your life will be impoverished. But if you wisely invest in beauty, it will remain with you all the days of your life"* --- Frank Lloyd Wright

As I mentioned in my introduction, the topics and general information were channeled through me. I also mentioned the connection to Lemuria. According to this information, it is now time to share with or re-introduce Lemuria to all living beings on the Earth Plane.

The Time of Lemuria is a period in our history where many species or cultures lived harmoniously upon this planet. The Lemuria societies were only one of many who came to the Earth. All were seeded from other places or planets. Whether they are called aliens, spirits or gods does not matter, each reader can choose the name of their choice.

Life at this time was a gentle period, filled only with love and harmony. Communication was telepathic which explains why there are no written records. For many of us today, it would appear that no one worked. Their work was simply different. What is important is their connection to Nature and the Arts. It is now time to explore this connection.

A person could stop at a particular tree or plant and would immediately know who had passed by and what thoughts were present. All relevant knowledge was immediately apparent to those passing. There was no need for books or records as we know them. However, their society included a role similar to our historians whose responsibility was ensuring that all knowledge and memories of special events was passed to future peoples.

Since music, painting and sculpting were integral parts of their life, this became the historian's medium. We will never know which came first -- the love of the arts leading to information within or the need for informational perpetuity leading to the love of arts. We do know though, that as the spread of Lemuria knowledge increases, we see a proliferation of the Arts in our present day living.

One of the first things archaeologists look for is evidence of fine arts. Weaving, painting and carving are all important in isolated indigenous cultures of today; they are simply gifts carried over from another time. The quantity and style of fine arts within a region, culture or even time period are all indications that the Earth is now ready to receive the information and wisdom being passed to us from the Time of Lemuria.

Today, we ask ourselves just how and why an entire culture disappeared. How was this knowledge coded so that eons later it could be deciphered? This is what I've been told:

> *...As the time of Lemuria was coming to an end and most entities were leaving, the Wise Ones knew that those staying behind would not use the information wisely. They did however realize that at some point in the distant future, there would be a need for their information. There were small groups of humans who would use it wisely. For them, the Wise Ones knew that a vague recollection of the wisdom remained, carried forward and remembered through myths and legends. For others the Wise Ones from Lemuria made plans for such a time when the door to their wisdom would open. They carefully stored the key to this door within the MANU NYMBA and in all nature.*

The love and respect of nature was maintained by those who remembered the vague link. Those people lost their telepathic ability but did not lose their love of nature or the arts. For others who returned or came to Earth they had to discover or find the information that was stored in the MANU NYMBA.

Earlier we stressed the minute size of the MANU NYMBA yet it exists in every corner of the cosmos and carries all knowledge. Choosing the MANU NYMBA was the logical option for the Wise Ones from Lemuria.

As the human race moved through time, there were various ways that these memories were stirred. Today, we look back and see the time line of awakening.

The first step was the myths and legends *remembered* by indigenous people. This is simply information of an unknown origin, carried forward by those who had a faint recollection of a past.

I compare this to a person today being drawn to a food, knowing they'll like it but also knowing they have never had it before. The indigenous knew at some level of their being that something was true.

The next step was herbal remedies, using parts of the plant for their healing properties. I wonder how healers so long ago knew certain plants healed certain ailments without extensive experimentation. This was long before the medical profession began around Descartes' time. Usually the remedies were prepared in teas or poultices which naturally required killing a part of the plant.

Here are examples of *the right time.* Modern societies are proud and claim to have discovered the concept of flower essences.

In the 1920s, an Englishman named Dr. Edward Bach reportedly discovered the properties of the *energy* of flowers. This required placing a flower in pure spring water out in the sunshine for a period of time. More than 40,000 years ago, the Aborigines in Australia were using flowers for healing. Legend tells us that Lemuria also used essences, the year is unknown.

Most practitioners follow the laborious process of placing a young, fresh blossom in pure water to gather the energy and healing properties. After the flower was removed, the pure spring water became the Mother tincture. Today, a growing number of people realize that it is not necessary to kill a blossom to gather the energy.

Since the MANU NYMBA, as the smallest part of life, resides on the surface of all parts of the plant such as the trunk, stem or blossom, it is not necessary to kill the life out of the plant. All that is needed is to take an air-tight container and slowly slide it over the surface; then fill the container with pure water. In this way, the energy is gathered, almost like taking scales off our skin.

This latter method allows us to bring the properties of sacred trees into our bodies without killing or harming the trees in any way. We can do this with the reverence they deserve.

Today, these remedies are made all around the globe and it is generally accepted that they can be used everywhere, not just in the place of original growth.

In my first book, INNER BRIDGES, I stressed the importance of matching food and remedies with the place of residency. Others now support this practice since a growing number realize that balance is important to our well-being. When an essence comes from another location it is not in balance with our body and therefore will not heal as quickly, but eventually it does restore.

I sense that we are being tested as humans to see if we can use the wisdom of herbs, essences and sacred trees responsibly. If this is so, then it won't be long before we will "remember" the ability of simply placing our hands on a plant for healing.

Someone asked me recently what happens in Northern climates where most plants sleep for half the year. How can we get the essence?

When I asked my guides, the answer I was given is that we can take a portion of the plant just before it goes to sleep and put it in a cold place, like a refrigerator. We can then run our hands over the leaves or bark, warming our hands later to absorb the plant's benefits into our body. The process of drying plants weakens the energy, making it ineffective for essences.

There are many books written on herbal remedies and flower essences, the valuable reference books come from the region where you live. Sources from the indigenous peoples of the region are also valuable. An encyclopedia containing a wide range of information is *The Encyclopedia of Flower Remedies by Clare G. Harvey and Amanda Cochrane.*

We are beginning an evolutionary step back to the time of Lemuria when all living entities carried all wisdom and healing needed. Shortly, we'll know how to access what is needed.

What Constitutes A Sacred Tree?

There are three forms of a sacred tree:

1. A regular physical tree
2. A shrub existing in a region where trees do not grow such as a desert or the cold north. There is always some form of a sacred life form for the inhabitants.
3. A symbolic tree such as the Tree of Life.

When we return to the myths and legends remembered by our peoples, the ones that probably have the most impact are the stories surrounding the sacred tree. All trees and natural life forms carry information, knowledge or telepathic records. We can only wonder in awe at the wisdom of the Lemuria residents. It appears that they ensured that no two living entities would carry the same information.

Information of the MANU NYMBA serves two purposes – maintaining the cultural memory of earth life and maintaining the CLP. They knew that when the time was right, residents of our planet would receive the correct information.

Since individual DNA and universal information is stored in ALL MANU NYMBA there are two resulting outcomes. To illustrate, let's divide the MANU NYMBA in imaginary left-right halves, each half carrying segments of both magnetic and electrical tetrahedrons.

The first half is responsible to the body, mind and spirit of a single entity. These three work together for the well-being of the individual soul and its cosmic family.

The second half carries the social or cultural memory. It is important to understand that should the MANU NYMBA be injured in any way, birth defects for example, the biggest loss would be the social memory.

The DNA and individual knowledge might be lost for one individual, but the biggest impact is the loss of social information; it is a total loss. It is this latter purpose that became known as Sacred Tree information.

It is this distant, almost forgotten memory of Lemuria that generated the reverence of nature on our planet.

All over the world, we find the mystification and deification of nature. The story details vary but there is a common theme behind the myths and stories about Sacred Trees. Yet, how did this happen? How did so many around the world *invent* or create similar tales?

Whether we believe that Lemuria was only a small continent or whether we believe it was large, encompassing most of the Pacific and Asia, the question of how the information traveled still exists.

One possibility is the variety of seeds picked up by migratory birds and planted elsewhere. Another possibility is that humans traveled to new lands with their faint memories intact. Whichever possibility the reader accepts, the knowledge went into the four corners of the world – NORTH, EAST, WEST, and SOUTH. We do know that the land masses of the world have shifted so the exact locations of the compass points are unknown. It is generally accepted the Lemuria was in the Pacific, placing the corners as:

- North to China, Mongolia and Inuit
- East to North and South America
- South to Australia
- West to India, Indonesia.

Migratory Paths of the human race

Without knowing anything about Lemuria or the scattering of seeds, anthropologists speculated that migration of people is responsible for common myths and legends. Perhaps this is so. Many people, including Thor Heyerdahl, proved that migration was possible. One theory placed a *bridge* from Asia to North America. Results varied with supporters for each theory.

The map below shows one theory, presenting migratory routes, marked in yellow lines.[5] This suggests all human life

---

[5] Microsoft® Encarta® Encyclopedia 2002. © 1993-2001 Microsoft Corporation, article on Race

began in Africa. What about the energy of plant life? How did seeds move around the planet? Are they carried by wildlife?

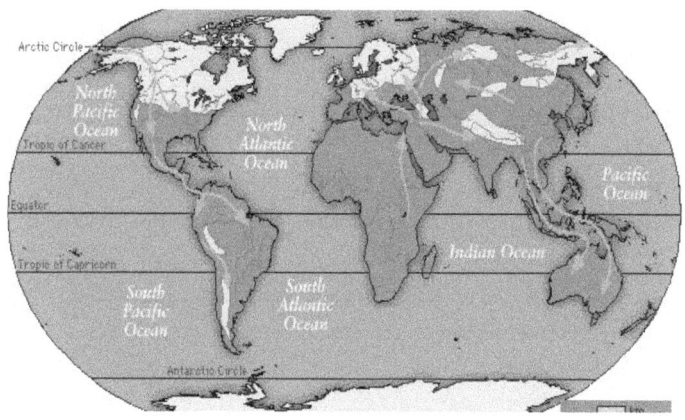

Scientists do not accept religious or metaphysical theories, but they have studied the migratory habits of wildlife. If a plant genus occurred around the world, then it could be said that *possibly* birds carried seeds on their migratory travels. Unfortunately, there is no evidence supporting this.

With an unsolved mystery on our hands, look at the myths and legends of **THE TREE OF LIFE** or **SACRED TREE** from various cultures and draw your own conclusions.

The Webster's New Collegiate Dictionary defines **MYTH** as:

> ...*a usually traditional story of ostensibly historical events whose origin has been lost.*

This Microsoft Encarta Encyclopedia defines **LEGEND** as:

> ...*a story coming from the past, esp. one regarded as historical although not verifiable.*

Both definitions state that they are historical but not provable.

What do we Gain?

According to the myths and legends from many cultures, we get:

1. Gifts giving life and health.
2. Special personal characteristics
3. Knowledge.
4. Guidance -- When asked, gods and goddesses help solve problems.
5. Life itself -- Should a specific tree die, then all life on Earth will die.

Looking back through history, there have been stories from all over the globe dating back to times when cultures or tribes lived in isolation. This is one of the strongest gifts from Lemuria.

Generally, cultures who revere trees usually worship multiple spirits or Gods. The exception, of course, is Christianity and Judaism. Christianity looks at the tree in the Garden of Eden that gave knowledge. Judaism looks at the Kabbalah. Both are relatively new religions and they concentrate on the acquisition of human characteristics.

Dr. Subash Chandran Madhav Gadgil MD Gadgil wrote an article on *Sacred Groves and Sacred Trees of Uttana Kannada* in a 1998 newsletter Indira Gandhi National Center for the Arts (IGNCA):

Dr. Gadgil said:

> *The concept of the sacredness of plants enters into every form of religion....It rests on the ear-*

liest conceptions of the unity of life in nature, in the sense of communion and fellowship with the divine center and the source of life.

This statement supports my latest information that many humans on this planet have a distant recollection of the bond between life forms.

The MANU NYMBA is the origin of life, therefore older than Lemuria. When we understand that Lemuria citizens had the ability to modify the MANU NYMBA and store information in it, then we also understand that they were capable of putting valuable information into the trees.

The Wise Ones had a very complex plan, they knew the information would become available when and where it was needed.

There are reports that the number of stray migratory birds and occasional sightings are escalating. Many blame humans for interfering with nature to such an extent that weather patterns change, hence migration.

Instead of blaming it just on altered weather patterns, perhaps it is simply the awakening of the Lemuria wisdom. Even the altered weather patterns may be information from the Time of Lemuria; the Wise Ones know when it is time.

These seeds have become part of the many myths of Sacred Trees and Trees of Life. Today, we get to enjoy the information from Lemuria, incorporating it into current life in the 21st century.

Creating Your Own Personal Sacred Tree

When we think of sacred trees, we tend to think globally, or at least culturally. However, many people do not feel comfortable adopting a Sacred Tree of another culture or part of the world.

I am frequently asked: "Will I be able to develop the connection with Lemuria without adopting another's tree?" The answer is yes. There is no reason why an individual or a family cannot have a personal sacred tree or bush. Each can create his or her own tree and gain their personal pathway to the Lemuria knowledge. Here is one way it can be done.

One of the purposes of a personal sacred tree is connecting the Earth and the Sky, thereby maximizing the energy that is available to those who choose to go to the tree.

Choosing to follow the instructions below would benefit *any* tree planting, whether it is in your own garden or by a community organization such as Scouts and Guides. The following is what I was told would generate the energy needed allowing a bush or tree to become a "SACRED TREE":

- *Dig the hole on the full moon. Digging the hole at full moon allows the moon to absorb the impurities from the hole. It also allows the Earth energy to move into the hole, ready for the plant to absorb the MANU NYMBA.*
- *Leave the hole empty until the new moon when the plant is placed in it. The new moon will then transfer its energy into the new plant.*
- *Meanwhile, collect water when the moon is waxing (two weeks prior to full moon). When the moon is on the wane (between full moon and new moon), cover the container to prevent the energy from dissipating. This keeps the water energized with the universal, lunar power.*
- *Between the full and new moon, sprinkle the hole with this water to ensure that the energy is maximized in the hole, the new home for the plant. By sprinkling the hole with the stored water, you are compensating for any energy loss occurring at the planting site.*

- *In addition to regular watering, at least twice a month, water the sacred tree with the energized water.*

ADOPTING A SACRED TREE FROM ANOTHER CULTURE

Various cultures and belief systems have their own myths and legends of sacred trees. Each is strong, sturdy enough to bond a group together. Today, we see a growing trend to adopt myths and legends into personal lifestyle.

An example that comes to mind is the interest in indigenous cultures. Unfortunately, many believe that because they are not indigenous, they cannot practice the ceremonial rites. This is not so. Whether an individual wants to delve into and follow a spiritual practice is a personal choice. Nevertheless, there is no reason why an individual cannot select a tree *they* consider sacred and call it their personal sacred tree.

There can be several reasons why someone may be drawn to myths beyond their heritage. One may be that their personal beliefs don't conform to their particular culture or group. Another reason for the intrigue is the desire to improve them. By incorporating myths into their life, they'll gain help acquiring specific characteristics.

Whatever the reason, we can all adopt a sacred tree from anywhere on the planet. We don't even have to plant it or water it!

To incorporate a sacred tree into our lives, we need to bring the energy into our lives, filling it with MANU NYMBA from our world. Setting up a structured display, or altar is the simplest process.

The method:

1. There are two main factors that are needed.
   a) We must bring the tree's energy into alignment with the region where we live. Blending the energies can be done either through symbolism or using a piece of the tree.
   b) A picture carries the best energy since it absorbs the complex interlocking of all the MANU NYMBA. To take the picture: take it at Full Moon. Place a glass of pure water and a lit candle nearby. It is important not to have any disturbing energy around. This is the quickest way to bring the tree's power into your world.
   c) Whether the bark, flower or fruit is dried or fresh, it is still a small segment of the total network of the MANU NYMBA. To get a complete image means that a map, as it were, must be built of the complete entity. If this is all that is available, it will work, just plan on allowing extra time.
   d) We need to boost the energy by placing images of both the MANU NYMBA and a crystal cluster inside the tree.
2. Select a location such as a table or altar for the center. It should be away from high activity in your home.
3. Place the symbol of your tree (picture, artifact or portion) in the center, toward the rear. Remember if you use a piece of the tree such as bark, leaf, fruit or flower, the setting cannot be disturbed for forty-eight hours.
4. If you are using a picture, *draw* or attach images of several interlocking MANU NYMBA across the

trunk of the tree including the meridian tubes. If you are using a piece of the tree, then pasting or sticking images on it is the easiest.
5. In front of the tree representative, there should be a MANU NYMBA with the crystal cluster at the base. The MANU NYMBA can be made out of whatever you choose, wire, plastic, clay, paper, etc. It's preferable to use a real quartz cluster rather than a picture to generate the energy.
6. Once the center is set up, it needs an initial clearing and then cleared regularly thereafter. Alternatives methods are:
    a) Lighting candles. This provides on-going clearing. Colors to match the MANU NYMBA are a good choice.
    b) Smudging defines what energies are allowed to stay.
    c) Ringing bells provide a gentle, clear sound that connects with the crystal. They also provide a color vibration which enhances the MANU NYMBA. Those who see colors will notice the shift. Others will notice the resulting calm.

There are many books detailing ways to set up a spiritual center or altar. All their techniques will work. Whatever they use as central focal point, we simply remove it and substitute the MANU NYMBA and crystal cluster.

The Life of Sacred Trees

For many people, spirituality can only be good. Since sacred trees are an integral part to spirituality, they must also be only good. In general, this is so. However, as our world becomes more polluted and there are many misguided souls upon our world, discrimination and trust become paramount. We can talk about a particular tree type as sacred and this will be so. This does not mean, however, that ALL trees of this type are sacred. This takes back to the old axiom that just because a statement is true in one way, this does not mean that the opposite is not always true. For example: If red is a color, then all color is red. How does this apply?

Trees have complex root and branch systems. When a tree grows in a healthy environment, then the roots and branches are all healthy, receiving everything that is needed for life. However, when a tree grow in an environment where pollution blows at it from one direction, then the branches on that side receive the pollution. Similarly, a root's function is to seek out nutrients, growing indiscriminately. As a root moves into toxic soil, it picks up toxins, carrying them through the entire plant. This particular tree may be sacred from a genus outlook but not from the individual perspective.

One image that kept appearing as I wrote this is the concept of caves, some friendly, full of purity and others foreboding, holding corruption. It is extremely important that we recognize that all trees, sacred or otherwise will hold these "caves". Once we begin to recognize energy that is not to our liking, we can adjust our plans, helping ourselves and the tree. Through this trust, we'll know which side of a tree is best for learning or healing. We'll also know when a tree's root system has picked up toxins.

As I prepared the text for this book, I kept "hearing" the name *Sycamore*. I finally looked it up. From numerous sources, I found the following information:

- The Sycamore is considered by some to be the biblical Tree of Life, believing it originated where Joseph set up his home
- Plato lectured his students under it.
- It grows in wet soil, often near wells
- They can live up to 500 years. At middle age, 200-300 years, they become hollow but still thrives
- Egyptians believed it held the spirits of the dead. It was sacred to Isis-Hathor goddesses.
- The Celts believed it to be a Money Tree
- It grows in Eastern States and North-Eastern Mexico.

Several additional items are pertinent:

1. The seeds have been carried around the globe with different varieties indigenous to different regions.
2. When it grows near wells, it can often be considered pure with little contamination.
3. The region and age are similar to the Ceiba Tree, sacred to the Mayan people.
4. MOST IMPORTANT: It carries all the attributes given to Sacred Trees around the world.
    a) Life and Health – good water.
    b) Eases stress, promotes revitalization
    c) Knowledge – Plato's wisdom
    d) Guidance – Linked to Christianity, Egyptian mythology and Celtic folklore

e) Life itself – Since it has similar properties to the Ceiba tree, possibly, it contains the beliefs of the Mayan.

If a single tree had to be chosen, the Sycamore is a complete package, carrying a complex system. The Lemuria people chose it as an information depository for the middle region of our globe.

World Myths of Sacred Trees

These many myths carry different origins and different emphasis. Some myths surround the meaning, or creation of life. Still others believe specific trees come from a higher source or house their deities. How peoples of the world and their myths refer to the Trees depends upon the time of the search and their culture.

The following is a delightful summary and prophecy written by Dr. Eusebius J. Mukhwana, Executive Director of SACRED Africa – **S**ustainable **A**griculture **C**enter for **R**esearch and Development in Africa.

Additional Information can be found on the following website: http://www.acts.or.ke/Reports/Sacred_Tree.html

It also clarifies

- Why is a sacred tree important?
- Why do we need to either create or adopt a tree of our own?
- Why do we need to go back to the information passed to us from Lemuria?

It said:

The Sacred Tree
(Adopted from the Forests, People and Trees newsletter)

Is a tree for all people, all tribes, clans and nations throughout Mother Earth.

Whose sacred visions, dreams, prayers, songs, wisdom, experience and guidance form the foundation and living reality for many in the world.

For all the people in the world, the Creator has planted a Sacred- Tree under which they all gather, and there find healing from the roots and bark, power to cook their food, wisdom and security.

The roots of the Sacred-Tree spread deep into the body of Mother Earth. An engagement that is mutual and permanent -- Peaceful co- existence.

Its branches spread upwards like hands praying for guidance and mercy. The fruits of the tree make meal for all of us at the end of the day. From this tree we learn love, compassion, generosity, patience, wisdom, justice, courage, respect, humility and caring for others.

The life of the tree is the life of the people, if the people wander far away from the protective and supportive shadow of the tree, if they forget to seek nourishment of its fruit, if they should turn against the tree and attempt to destroy it,

> *great sorrow and suffering will fall upon the people.*
>
> *Many will become sick at heart. They will lose their power. They will cease to dream and have visions. They will start to quarrel among themselves over worthless trifles. They will be unable to tell the truth and to deal with each other honestly. They will watch themselves and their offspring perish from the excesses of their lives. They will turn against each other, each blaming the other for their miseries.*
>
> *It is foretold that these things will come to pass, but the life of the Sacred-Tree will never cease.*
>
> *A day will come, when the people will awaken, as if from a long, drugged sleep and will begin, timidly a first, but later with great urgency to search again for solutions to their problems. In doing this, they have to find the Sacred-Tree again. The knowledge about its whereabouts and the fruits that adorn its branches have always been carefully guarded and preserved among the minds and hearts of our wise elders.*
>
> *These humble, simple, loving and dedicated souls will guide anyone who is honestly and sincerely seeking along the path leading to the protective shadow of the Sacred Tree...*

Because of the complexity of this section, there is a detailed summary of only one tree from each of the four directions plus a few names of other trees in each direction. The purpose however shows both the scope and the similarity of the stories.

When your interest is pulled to a specific tree, check out a detailed book in your library or a Web Site for additional information. Some of my sources were:

1. Tree Mythology http://www.members.aol.com/birchfire/TreesUZ.html
2. Yggdadrasil http://www.owlsdottir.com/elements/trees/sacredtree.html
3. Origins and Variations of the Sacred Tree http://assyria.nineveh.com/sacred.html
4. Myths of the Sacred Tree, http://www.gotoit.com/titles/mysatr.html

NORTH
- China, North America, Scandinavia, Germany

EAST
- Central America, Maya, Greece

SOUTH
- Australia, New Zealand

WEST
- India, Indonesia

THE NORTH

China

The Chinese revere ALL old trees, not necessarily just one species. The one exception would be the **GINKGO BILOBA**, regarded as one of the oldest trees. They have used its properties to enhance health, ***long-life and wisdom*** for more than 3,000 years. This is also the herb used today for mental acuity and anti-aging -- what better gifts from Lemuria. The Lemuria people are known for living long lives and their mental acuity was reportedly beyond our comprehension.

Since the Chinese believe old trees absorb energy from the environment, this is probably why the Bonsai is so popular. Having an old tree nearby balances the Yin/Yang of their personal living space. Since they also believe that good spirits live in old trees and will help all who worship, they can guarantee **guidance** from them right in their home.

According to a good friend, Dr. Damon Lee, TCM Practitioner,[6] who lived in both Mainland China and Hong Kong prior to moving to Canada, the following are memories of sacred trees in his life in China.

The Yung tree

Often called the "Wishing tree", this king tree grows throughout South-East Asia. One of the most popular specimens grows in the New Territory, Hong Kong, estimated to be about 100 years old, not very old compared to the Ginkgo trees. Nevertheless, these trees are revered and considered to be spiritual because they are so old and large. Often you will see many colorful paper bags with red string hanging all over it. When a person throws the bag against the tree, catching it upon the tree branches, legend has it that the person's wishes will become true.

Rural Life

Almost every community in rural China almost has an old tree in the center of a courtyard. There, residences burn incense

---

[6] http://www.holisticmasters.com Dr. Damon Lee

and red long candles with bamboo sticks and paper money. A small temple, approximately 3' x 4' is built next to the tree housing two elder figures. These clay or wood figures are considered minority Gods who are the guardians of the temple. In addition to incense and candles burning you will find offerings of food. When a wish is fulfilled, more elaborate offerings such as barbequed pig, cakes, steamed chickens, are brought to the tree as a way of saying thanks to the spirits.

NORTH AMERICA

Pacific Northwest

Indigenous people throughout North America have revered nature with trees in particular. The **Cedar** is the center of their culture which is one of the oldest trees, and as such is part of many of their ceremonies. They "smudge" with cedar and sage to remove unwanted spirits and welcome in others.

Placing bows of cedar under the pillow enhances dreamtime **knowledge.** This practice also helps with internal cleansing for **health and long life**.

The Lakota Indians

The Lakota people in the United States consider the **Cottonwood** as their Tree of Life. **If it dies, so will all other life die.** The **Poplar** tree is used for ceremonial dancing. The outcome would differ depending upon the purpose of the dance.

SCANDINAVIA

YGGDRASIL: The Norse Tree of the Universe

Like the Maya, the Scandinavian and Germanic people had a world tree that represented the universe with the roots and limbs spreading everywhere. Their choice for this tree was the **Ash** tree.

The **Yggdrasil**, passed through all realms, very much like the connection of Body, Mind, and Spirit of our present world. The central trunk, or Heart line, carried the strengths of all three. We can compare the central trunk with the Chinese Meridian system or the MANU NYMBA system with the meridian tubes; one more similarity. The description of the mythology is detailed and complex. Odin has been quoted as saying:

> *"No one has ever known or will ever know the vastness of the roots of that ancient tree."*

Germany

When Germanic people joined the Norse in the Scandinavian world, they considered the **Ash** Tree as sacred. This gives us four gifts from Lemuria –

- Nourishment
- Healing,
- Protection
- Luck

THE SOUTH

Australia

The **Baobab** tree is native to Australia and Madagascar, an island just off Africa. It is known to live from 2,000 to 6,000 years. It also has a hollow trunk, like the Sycamore and the Ceiba trees. For this reason, large amounts of water can be stored within its trunk. The peoples who have lived with this tree learned to use every part of it. It gives **health** through medicinal properties. It gives **personal characteristics** such as fertility.

New Zealand – Maori

There are many myths and legends about the two Maori trees. The legend of the **Pohutukawa** tree tells of a young man who tried to avenge his father and fell to the Earth, thereby creating the tree. For thousands of years, the placenta of a baby was placed upon the tree and watched over. This ensured the **health** of the young person. They also used boiled bark to heal sores and stop bleeding.

Since the blossoms were red, it was believed that an angry person could sit under the tree to ease their anger by transferring the redness or flushed skin back to the red flower.

The **Rata** tree was supposed to guard a cave where the spirits or souls went. By protecting the entrance kept the souls safe and after that, people could seek **guidance** from the departed.

THE WEST

Since Lemuria is the source of knowledge, we are taking the compass points from the Pacific, one of their suspected locations. Therefore India is to the West, not East as the presumed Eastern lands from European countries.

Living in Lemuria, Maya becomes East, not the assumed West.

India

In India the **Jambu** Tree is worshiped as the extension of Shiva, one of their Gods. It is supposed to produce the drink of **immortality**. I suspect this is why it is one of the legendary trees where Buddha gained insight and **wisdom.** The name Jambu refers to the Guava, *Jambu biji* or the Rose Apple, *Jambu Air*. These fruits are believed to give **long life and good health to all,** containing the pertinent healing properties.

The Hindu also respects the Asvotha and the Pippala, both known for their **healing** properties. Asvotha also generates **wisdom**.

We cannot finish a discussion about India without speaking of the **Bodhi** Tree. This is the tree where Buddha received his enlightenment and therefore is attributed with **knowledge** and **guidance.**

Indonesia

For them, the **Banyan** Tree is sacred because of the springs found at the base of the trees. It is believed that holy spirits live there, ensuring the availability of **clean water**. For the

Javanese people of Java, sacred spirits dwell within the forests, close to the Banyan trees.

THE EAST

Central America –Mayan People

The Maya is an ancient culture, once thriving and widespread. Today, only a small number remain scattered over several countries, from the Yucatan Peninsula in Mexico south through Belize, Guatemala, Honduras and El Salvador.

Their culture was divided into small states, speaking approximately 30 languages. In spite of this diversity, the central tree for all was the **Ceiba** Tree, also known as Wakah Kan. To the Maya the tree represents the universe. Above the Earth, it was the heavens. The branches reached out to the skies searching for **knowledge** and **guidance.** The trunk represented both man on earth and the Milky Way in the sky, the axis of life.

It is from the trunk that the people received strength Like the Sycamore tree, the trunk became hollow as the tree grew older. The roots were the underworld where all souls went and lived.

For Maya culture, this tree gave all gifts – **health, personal traits, knowledge, guidance** and **life itself.** They believed that to get what they wanted or needed, all they had to do was make a sacrifice or offering to the appropriate god through the Ceiba Tree.

GREEK MYTHOLOGY

Sacred Trees were an integral part of Greek Mythology, connecting many trees and Gods.

This is possibly the only culture who did not revere just one tree. Instead they linked Gods and attributes with different trees. This differs from the Chinese who respected ALL old trees.

Many consider Greece to be one of the forerunners of modern Western Society; their mythology impacting today's world.

According to Greek beliefs, each tree carries traits from the MANU NYMBA. Below is a table of the Greek Gods, the trees, and the attributes associated with each one. The MANU NYMBA reference is in italics, enclosed in brackets.

Trees	**Greek Gods**	**Characteristic & MANU NYMBA link**
OAK	Zeus	Ruler, Justice *(Sun-Leadership)*
WILLOW	Hera	Patron of Marriage *(Pluto-Relaxation)*
OLIVE	Athena	Wisdom & Warfare *(Mercury—Wisdom)*
LAUREL	Apollo	Arts, Prophecy & Medicine *(Neptune—healing)*
PINE	PAN	Protector of flocks *(Mars—Love & Harmony)*
POPLAR	Hercules	Strength *(Saturn—stability)*

EAST -- WEST

Generally, when people hear the words *Sacred Tree* or *Tree of Life*, they immediately think of either Christianity or Judaism.

In Christianity, the tree of knowledge in the Garden of Eden and the tree chosen for the cross at Jesus' crucifixion are both sacred.

In Judaism, the Kabbalah explains the Jewish doctrine in the form of a tree, hence the Tree of Life.

Since both religions originated in the Middle East, I am placing the Tree of Life in a section by itself where East meets West.

The Kabbalah Tree of Life

Perhaps the most popular tree is the Sacred Tree or Tree of Life from the Jewish Qabbalah; spoken of in Genesis book of the Bible. David Allen Hulse makes the following comments:

> *The Babylonian-Assyrian Tree of Life (usually composed of 13 fruits joined by bent and straight Paths) can be seen as the prototype for this Jewish Tree of Life. The Greek tetractys, a four tiered pyramid of ten dots, can also be seen as a source of the Qabalistic Tree of Life.*
>
> *A unique symbol for the number series 1 through 10 was developed out of the Jewish Kabbalah from the symbolism in Genesis. The Tree of Life that grew in the center of Eden became the mandala or symbolic pattern used to describe the mysticism behind the first ten numbers.... It is typically composed of ten cir-*

> *cles (known as Sephiroth connected by a series of straight lines known as Paths).*
>
> *Ultimately, the shape of the Tree of Life developed into a circle surmounting a cross, resembling both the Egyptian Ankh and the medieval astrological symbol for Venus (both symbolic of life).*[7]

The graph and table below shows the traditional Sacred Tree with the 10 Sephiroth and the meanings behind the 10 circles.

The Sephiroths represent the states of consciousness or way of being. The *branches* lead to transition or change.

This information is basic to Kabbalah study. I came across many different spellings for the Hebrew words. I chose what seems to be the most popular. Many readers are not fluent in Hebrew; therefore I attached the English definitions.

---

[7] Hulse, David Allen, "The Eastern Mysteries", Llewellyn Publications, St. Paul, MI, 2000, Pg.35

WITHIN & BEYOND: REVISITED

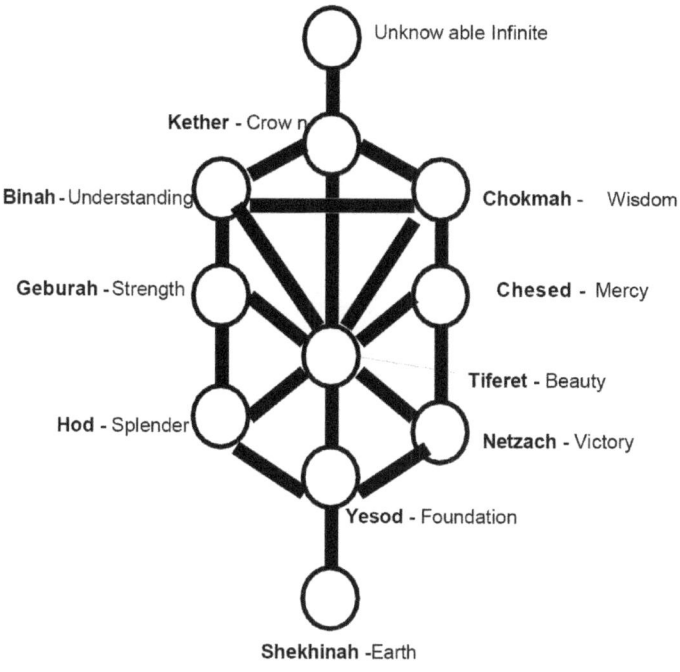

THE TREE OF LIFE & THE 10 SEPHIROTHS

Names in Hebrew	**Characteristics in English**
Kether	Divine Crown
Binah	Understanding
Chokmah	Wisdom
Geburah	Strength
Chesed	Mercy
Tif'eret	Beauty
Hod	Splendor
Netzach	Victory
Yesod	Foundation
Shekhinah	Earth elements

Cross Reference
Sephiroth names and related characteristics

According to the Kabbalah study, the left side of the Tree gives the **female** traits of power and strict justice. The right side identifies the **masculine** traits of unity, harmony and benevolence. The **middle sephiroths** give the ideal balance of mercy and justice.

As I channeled the information for the first section of this book, I had little knowledge about Sacred Trees other than the name and general interpretation. Later, as I wrote this portion of the book, I repeatedly heard the words MANU NYMBA.

This indicates that there is a connection somewhere between the two; Tree of Life and the MANU NYMBA. Consequently, I looked at the two and found interesting correlations. This is not a precise match but they warrant comment.

For a visual comparison, I had to *pinch* the tree in the middle, providing a close comparison. This is followed by a table providing the same information, just different format.

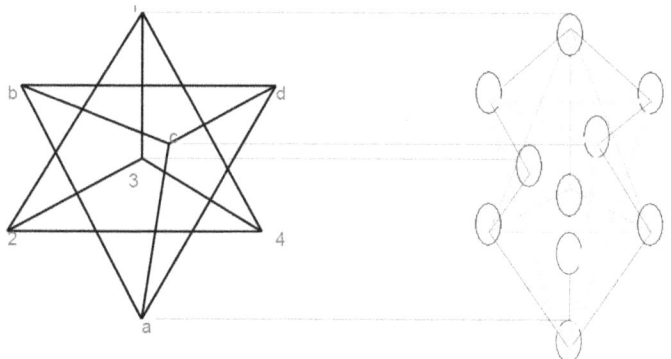

Comparison of MANU NYMBA and the TREE OF LIFE

The Sun Tetrahedron (electrical) is indicated by numbers. The Earth Tetrahedron (magnetic) is marked with lower case letters.

Table Comparison of MANU NYMBA and TREE OF LIFE

	MANU NYMBA		TREE OF LIFE	
1	Chiron	Intuition	Kether	Divine Crown
2	Venus	Dignity	Hod	Splendor
3	Uranus	Spiritual	Tif'eret	Beauty
4	Jupiter	Bravery	Netzach	Victory
a	Saturn	Stability	Yesod	Foundation
b	Mercury	Wisdom	Binah	Understanding
c	Sun	Leadership	Chesed	Mercy
d	Mars	Love & Harmony	Chokmah	Wisdom

It becomes a personal choice whether you, as a reader, prefer the graphic sketch or the reference table. Either way, there are similarities or differences between the two tetrahedrons.

In some definitions, you might find that items match traditional descriptions while in other cases, they are slightly different. An example, number **2** and letter **d** motivate the reader to pause for thought.

These definitions and classifications come from the Spirit guides.

When we compare the traits of the tree of Life according to the MANU NYMBA structure, this is the cornerstone of our existence.

The skills, then, are

Magnetic
Foundation
Understanding
Mercy
Wisdom

Electrical
Divine
Crown
Splendor
Beauty
Victory

The Kabbalah Tree of Life dates back to biblical times, the book of Genesis. According to the story, it was passed to Abraham from God through an angel. These stories developed into religion.

Ancient indigenous cultures also had stories developing into spirituality.

All the stories had both angels and legends, just with different names.

Angels, legends, religion and spirituality all require trust and belief in the unknowable. Until such time that humans remember what was true, this is the best way to keep the seeds alive.

First, we have a Spiritualist Church. Secondly, there are personal beliefs.

A Spiritualist Church has no fixed creed or dogma Spiritual Healing, Mediumship and Messages from Spirit form the foundation of their community They welcome everyone to open their hearts and minds in the ongoing search to understand our human and spiritual natures.

Secondly, there are personal beliefs in spirits and guides in contrast to structured religion. It tends to be a structured belief in spirits and divine guidance but places it within *organized* structure.

It is this organized structure that altered the scope of information available to all humans. It is difficult for religion to survive without a power and egotistical structure. Spirituality lives continually.

This alters information as it is discovered, eliminating religion as a reliable avenue for passing information. Fortunately, there were other doors.

Throughout history, we have seen the wisdom of the spiritual and healing properties of trees passed on through song, verbal tales and the writing. Since humans couldn't remember how these properties evolved out of our MANU NYMBA, they had to rely on the accuracy of their tools. Today, we are seeing different tools being discovered. We discover mysterious crop circles, inscrutable crystal skulls and cryptic signs and symbols all being unearthed.

Through these, we will begin to discover a multitude of information about the MANU NYMBA. Many doors are opening.

SIGNS --TOOLS FOR COMMUNICATION

> *"Good communication is as stimulating as black coffee and just as hard to sleep after."* Anne Morrow Lindbergh

We are living in what is called **The Information Age**. Generally, this title refers to computer technology. However for the spiritual mind, the term "information" goes beyond the computer or telephone.

Historically, the information time-line might be oral sagas, then rhymes and legends, leading to pictographs and finally through to petroglyphs. This led to information being stored in art forms then books and finally in computer memory.

Over time, knowledge took a broad swing from right-brain art over to left-brain activity.

While the original depositories were creative, they were just as dependent upon belief systems, analytical verbal acuity and storage. The true Information Age needs to integrate the left-brain functions with the right brain activities of intuition and spatial thinking.

It is time to integrate the wisdom coming from our distant past and the spirit world without the fear associated with analytical and judgmental thinking. It will be a challenging task and to achieve this two things are required.

The first requirement is larger receptacles of wisdom readily available to all living beings. Books are useful, and limited, only if a person could read a certain language. A legend restricted to a select group becomes no longer appropriate. Today, we need to have all knowledge available to ALL humanity.

An individual cannot learn how to access the information until they understand the wisdom and responsibility that goes with this privilege. Our trust in this development is imperative. Fortunately, most people working with ancient wisdoms today understand the responsibility and do not abuse the power.

Over time, we gradually divided our understanding into three categories of knowledge and these are cosmic, universal and societal wisdom.

The cosmic is in our DNA. To accept the key to cosmic knowledge, we go *within* our body to the MANU NYMBA.

Universal and societal knowledge come from *beyond* our body in one of three places:

1. CRYSTAL SKULLS
2. SACRED TREES
3. EARTH DESIGNS.

We need to know how to work with tools such as language, coding or symbology. When the crystalline cluster is balanced and growing as it should, we are able to interpret all ancient knowledge.

Life on the earth, including the earth itself is crystal. Knowing where the information is stored is of little use until we learn how to work with the tools; the second most important piece of information.

The MANU NYMBA gives us an inner knowing that is available through meditation, reviewed earlier. However, it is imperative that when your objective is to access your MANU NYMBA information, the intent of the meditation must be clearly stated as you go into the meditation.

Information from Sacred Trees and Crystal Skulls is obtained either through meditation, standing beside an object, holding, or touching the object. This information comes through pictorial images, sound or visionary signs.

When you begin to receive the latter, they will be in one of two shapes, or a combination. These are *Cuneiform* shapes or *Soft Curves*.

Cuneiform shapes provide information from the past on Earth.

Soft Curves give data from other planets and spirit guides.

Cuneiforms are a style of writing used through ancient Western Asia and indigenous cultures, consisting of straight lines formed into wedge-shaped patterns. This style of writing attributed to the Sumerians, dates back more than 5,000 years. A checkmark "√" could be considered a modern cuneiform. The Soft curves are gentle and transitory. An s-shape curve "*S*" is an example.

The dollar sign "$" is an example of a modern day combination sign. Many ancient languages such as Sanskrit, Tibetan, Chinese, and Japanese use combinations of cuneiforms and soft curves for their written language.

Today, we interpret their written language simply as a communication tool. However, we must remember that long ago, the wise ones knew the importance of keeping their historical and their universal information accessible to their descendants. The individual letters may simply appear as a form of writing to our modern world but in reality, they contain so much more information.

WITHIN & BEYOND: REVISITED

Signs can be directional, flowing from the top down, the bottom up, the left or the right. Markings over or under the letter indicate the same thing. Ancient languages required the letters to be written in a specific order. If they were written in the reverse direction, the meaning changed. This is not so with English. English flows in one direction. Have we gradually separated ourselves from the knowledge and blocked this simple reminder? How the images appear when we *receive* them tells us whether it is either cosmic or planetary energy; both necessary and valuable. It is possible to receive a sign with planetary energy in the middle of cosmic signs. It is simply a combination or clarity of data. I am reminded of an English sentence with a foreign word in the middle, giving clarity. The speaker is choosing the best to tell a story.

Using the word 'receive' often causes some confusion. If I had used the word 'see', some readers would expect literally to see a sign with their physical eyes. However, this is not always the case. Yes, there are times when you will see the sign or shape appearing in cloud formations or as images in the trees. Most of the time though, they come to you in a meditation or a dream and not everyone sees three dimensionally in their dreams. Whether you 'see' or 'receive' them through another sense is very personal trait.

However, since they are usually graphical rather than auditory, seeing is a more accurate term. It does not matter whether you see them through your eyes or imagination. What is important is discovering how the signs appear to you. This wisdom allows you to use them as an oracle or conversely, as a means of communication – the most powerful.

What is important is that the more balanced your MANU NYMBA is, the more signs you are likely to receive. Learning to automatically merge the MANU NYMBA and the crystalline cluster into one thought form better enables us to receive and interpret more signs. Crystals are a tool of communication and an integral part of our being.

Mankind has developed many methods, the spoken word, written word and hand signals. All these are nothing more than a translator tool of the original message, which arrived through the crystals within us and on the planet.

The information gathers in our conscious being, which had to be transferred from our physical being. Here are a few signs or symbols that came to me through meditation or other methods

There are many keys to opening the gateway for signs and symbols; one is utilizing pillars or obelisks with your meditations. The following is one example:

Take a moment now or just before you begin meditation and place your hands at your side with the palms facing up. Close your eyes and focus your attention on the palms of the hands. Soon you will become aware of energy rays coming into the palms. This is the main beam of universal energy flowing into your body; the protection we require. This brings in one half of the MANU NYMBA.

This method can also be combined with the Asian spiritual mantra – OM.

It is a standard process to envelop the body with a bubble of white light. Long ago, somewhere on the globe it evolved to become the best procedure, so the system development and expanded.

Complete protection and connection comes in two rays or pillars made in a very soft gold-white light.

Throughout this golden light are filmy images of signs appropriate for each person. Again, how the signs are received varies according to the individual.

For example, they may appear as soft coloration of the ray, looking like a jet stream or bank of clouds in the sky. Another way may be different colors flowing in and out of the gold beam.

You must remember that the method will be whatever makes sense to the individual. This is why it is so important to learn your personal way of seeing the signs.

Here is an example of a plaster pillar with images painted on each side.

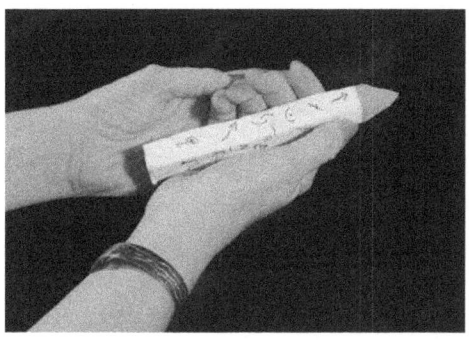

Historically as people learned of these pillars of light, the need to show off their knowledge and ownership of personal signs grew. Although signs may differ from one person to another, they are NOT exclusive to an individual.

This initiated the tradition of placing pillars or obelisks at the gates of their homes or in courtyards. Over time, this practice came to symbolize power and prestige; Egypt is an example.

For some time obelisks or pillars appeared in meditations, interspersed with information about various signs, but no lucidity. Finally an answer came; an answer for the human mind.

> *The pillars are very important because they tell other spirits the status of those who use them. When two pillars stand outside a home or are received in a meditation, they indicate an important family. Lesser families used only one. When there is a single row of in-line pillars, they are seen as a single guardian.*

This concept of status or the superiority of any one human or spirit can be bothersome because of the belief that every soul, at different times has lived in all levels of society. The information arrives to us today in such a way that those living in 21st century will understand.

For the visual reader, seeing an energy beam as a message board might be difficult whereas visualizing a personal obelisk or signpost is not.

Just as each beam of energy flowing into a body is different, so are the obelisks; each soul or entity has their own. When we are ready to use this as a communication tablet for the signs, we have a couple of decisions.

Will it be a beam of gold light or an obelisk?

If we choose the obelisk, will it come as a two dimensional drawing on paper? Will we create a tangible three-dimensional one; or will we simply imagine it?

Whatever approach, they both open doors for information. They can then be used in several ways:

1. As a meditation tool to ask for general information. As an oracle, this is powerful because you can get what you need at any particular time.
2. As another method for *sending* messages to your guides, an alternative to telepathy.

3. When you receive the signs through meditations, you can look for the same symbols in your environment. Once you understand the meanings, these locations will make sense, giving you even more information.

Meaning of numbers

When a new study is started, people tend to concentrate on a single aspect of the subject. When this happens, it means that the concentration is on the meaning of the signs, ignoring other information. While this is the central theme, there are other details not to be ignored. It is like reading only the noun or verb in a sentence. A general idea is picked up but much is missed.

One additional detail is the number of signs that appear. It is not uncommon to see the same or similar signs at the same time or several days in a row. These may appear individually or they may appear in a line. Ask yourselves – "Why did so many of this particular sign appear at this time? What does this quantity mean?"

For instance if the first sign displayed is what is shown below as #5 (⌐⌐), it provides limited information. If it appears more than once, it could be telling you several things.

It may be telling you that you need to take some action before receiving more information.

Possibly, you need to concentrate on balancing your body before it is ready to receive more information.

Most of us have an affinity for one number over the others. This number is more important than interpreting the meaning through an outside, recognized school of thinking. If you have not given much thought to the meaning of your *lucky* number, then pause and reflect upon the events occurring in your life when you noticed your number.

For those who choose to go beyond their personal lucky number to find a number's meaning there are many options.

Religions provide interpretations.

Esoteric studies such as Kabbalah, Astrology, and Tarot also provide us with interpretations.

If one particular topic intrigues you, I encourage independent study. Until then, the following should suffice.

It becomes important not to simply scan various systems' definitions searching for a meaning that suits them. The human mind is very adept at playing this game. For example, when we look at the two Mayan meanings for the number three we can see "Rhythm – movement, flow" or "Intensity – increasing in strength." Often we would prefer to have a rhythm in our lives than an intense situation.

If we have been following the second, then that is the meaning we need. Do you keep going to various doctors until you get an answer you like? Jumping around does not always provide accuracy.

MANU NYMBA

The MANU NYMBA gives the equivalent of eight numbers, four for each tetrahedron. Replacing the alphanumeric designations with all numeric labels, we see these numbers with the following definitions.

Points

Electrical
1. Intuition

2. Dignity
3. Spiritual
4. Bravery

Magnetic
1. Stability
2. Wisdom
3. Leadership
4. Love & Harmony

When the signs appear in a regular frequency, we need to pay attention to one of these three messages; depending on how many times the sign appears:

1. The trait is important for understanding the sign
2. What we need to focus on to bring balance into our being
3. Repeat the sign this many times.

The question to ask is: "How will I know what is accurate for me?" The answer usually comes either by going into meditation or using a pendulum with the sign and asking the question.

Mayan Study:

Numbers are very important in the Maya culture. Beliefs and religion center on time and calendar, mathematically complex and accurate. Since each community was isolated, the interpretations varied slightly from one to the next. They all used 17 different calendars, each with a base of 13.

People spend years studying these systems before fully understanding the meaning of numbers to them. Fortunately for us neophytes, some scholars put their knowledge to use and developed oracle decks. These decks now give us an accurate interpretation of numbers.

For more information, personal study with a specific deck is available in these two Mayan references:

- **The Mayan Oracle** by <u>Ariel Spilsbury & Michael Bryner</u>.
- **The Wisdom of the Maya** by <u>Dr. R.L. Bonewitz</u>

There are discrepancies between the two lists, perhaps originating from the differences in regions in the Mayan world.

To gain a thorough understanding of numerical meaning, stay with one system for a while. Later, if it does not seem to fit, then switch.

<u>Numbers</u>	<u>Mayan Oracle interpretation</u>
One	Unity – unconditional love
Two	Polarity – cooperation, relationships
Three	Rhythm – movement, flow
Four	Measure – order, natural cycles
Five	Center – core purpose or intent
Six	Organic balance – receptivity, ability to respond
Seven	Mystical Power – alignment, self-acceptance
Eight	Harmonic Resonance – path of the heart
Nine	Greater cycles – completion, expansion
Ten	Manifestation – intention, motivation, true identity
Eleven	Dissonance – change, disintegration

Twelve	Complex Stability – expansion, connectedness
Thirteen	Universal Movement – unexpected change

Numbers	**Wisdom of the Maya**
One	New beginning – emergence
Two	Intensity – unseen, creative forces giving life
Three	Intensity, a little stronger than two, opening of the spirit world
Four	Support – material sustainers of life
Five	Strength, building block
Six	Passing of old, outmoded things
Seven	Sudden opportunities
Eight	Crisis but cardinal support
Nine	Go within, cleanse and purify
Ten	Powerful support, moving forward
Eleven	Health, sexuality
Twelve	Little worries
Thirteen	Universal energy

Runes:

The cuneiform design of the Runes probably originated with the Greek or Roman cultures. Unlike these two cultures, the Vikings had neither paper nor writing instrument; carving cuneiform images on stone or trees was the only option.

At various times in history, the number of runes in their alphabet ranged from 16 to 24 runes. Later in the cuneiform section, we will talk more about these signs. At this point, however, it is the mythical legend accompanying the runes that is relevant.

According to legend, Odin, the Norse god speared himself to a tree attempting to discover the knowledge and mysteries of the runes. Because of this, the Vikings believe Runes possess divine and magical powers. Today, there are various oracles based on this mythology. There are usually 25 runes making up the entire oracle system. Interspersed throughout the system are 13 runes defined as the *Cycle of initiation or self-change.*

Just as we viewed the numerical interpretations of other systems, we can look at this cycle to gain one more perspective. The following is a list of the 13 runes, their names and their meanings taken from **The Book of Runes** by Ralph Blum.

I separated the numbering so that you can see the cycle runes as a group, not interspersed. Other sources have similar meanings.

Number	**Viking name**	**Meaning**
3-	Anuz --	Signals, the messenger
4	Othila	Separation, Retreat, Inheritance
5	Uruz	Strength, Manhood/Womanhood
6	Perth	Initiation, something hidden
7	Nauthiz	Constraint, necessity, pain
8	Inguz	Fertility, new beginnings
14	Kano	Opening, fire
16	Berkana	Growth, Rebirth
17	Ehwaz	Movement, progress
19	Hagalaz	Disruptive natural forces, elemental power
20	Raido	Communication, union, reunion
21	Thurisaz	Gateway, place of non-action
22	Dagaz	Breakthrough, transformation

The other important 11 runes are:

1	Mannaz	Willingness to change self
2	Gebo	Partnership
9	Eihwaz	Block defeat and stress
10	Algiz	Protection
11	Fehu	Fulfillment
12	Wunjo	New energy, blessings
13	Jera	Harvest rewards
15	Teiwaz	Go with Universal energy
18	Laguz	Immerse in living
23	Isa	At a standstill
24	Sowelu	Wholeness, completion

Arithmomancy

Arithmomancy is an offshoot of numerology. There are several dependable reference books. This information came from the book by Julia Line -- *The Numerology Workbook,* published by Aquarian Press

Pythagoras developed a comprehensive letter/numerical interpretation. Although this system includes specific meanings for larger numbers than 20, they are excluded and lower numbers are studied since the frequency of a signs appearance is only applicable to lower numbers. Good book on numerology should also have similar descriptions.

1. Ambition, passion, purpose
2. Ruin, fatality
3. The recognition of God, soul and destiny
4. Wisdom, strength and power
5. Marriage, happiness

6. Perfected labor
7. Happiness
8. Justice and protection
9. Worry, fallibility
10. Success and future happiness
11. Discord, evasion, lack of integrity
12. City, town, name
13. Injustice
14. Sacrifice, generosity
15. Kindness and integrity
16. Love, happiness and integrity
17. Carelessness
18. Selfishness and callousness
19. Foolishness
20. Wisdom and asceticism

Looking at these numbers as they relate to signs, what is going on in the physical life is pertinent. For example, if a sign shows up four times we can see it from two sides.

The first time means either "continue with your project or direction, it will bring strength and power".

If you go in the direction the sign suggest, you will need all your strength and power, stop and analyze. Both are correct but personal variables need to be applied.

In addition to the interpretations outlined above, Pythagoras introduces the qualities of numbers one to nine, often as many as ten traits for some numbers. Below are six qualities per number, three each for the positive and negative key words.

Pythagorean Number Qualities

#	Positive Traits	Negative Traits
1	Pioneering, powerful, creative	Intolerant, obstinate, egotistical
2	Emotional, Understanding, balance	Deceitful, cruel, malicious
3	Versatile, artistic, witty	Frivolous wasteful, outspoken
4	Steady, calm, practical	Dull melancholic, suspicious
5	Adventurous, clever, resourceful	Conceited, sarcastic, nervous`
6	Domesticated, reliable, harmonious	Complacent, trivial, selfish
7	Mystical, intellectual, secretive	Lazy, aloof, dreamy
8	Materialistic, tough, tenacious	Obstinate, ruthless, unscrupulous
9	Humanitarian, impulsive, unorthodox	Intolerant, deceptive, uncharitable

Astrology:

Astrology can be an effective interpretive tool. The key is noting the significant numbers that appear and applying them to your personal life. Usually that aspect of your life needs to be studied.

We cannot assume a single number means something specific, only that it pertains to some part of your life.

Where it would be useful is if you saw the number of a particular sign. Then, I would take the meaning of the sign as it applies to that aspect of your life. For example if #13 showed up three times, I would look at your inner balance as it pertains to your immediate environment.

There are 12 astrological houses.

The first three houses are the basic foundations and explorations of the self and individual interests.

The fourth, fifth and sixth houses look at these same basic foundations and how they apply to our interaction with others and the shared interests.

The next three houses, seven, eighth and ninth deal with expanded experiences, worldly concerns and how they affect our interactions with others.

The last three houses also deal with expanded experiences and world concerns but now look at how they relate to our inner exploration.

Individual House Definitions

1st House: Looks at how this applies to the **Self** -- Who are you?

2nd House: Looks at **personal worth, skills and Resources.** What value am I?

3rd House: Looks at how this applies in the **Immediate Environment**

4th House: Looks at **Position in the home or family**

5th House: Looks at **Shared creations.** What do I contribute?

6th House: Looks at **Daily life**. What energy do I expend?

7th House: Looks at the **Interaction with others**. What are my relationships like?

8th House: Looks at the **Shared resources**. How do my skills blend with other's skills?
9th House: Looks at **Expanded horizons**.
10th House: Looks at our place in the **Social structure** of our lives.
11th House: This house looks at **Future visions**. What visionary possibilities exist?
12th House: This house looks at our **Spiritual life** and how can we adapt and change who we are.

The Signs and Their Meanings

I call the years 1999 to 2002 the years of the signs, or symbols. Over this time, I received more than 40 different signs, both cuneiforms and soft curve shapes. I was shown pillars with images; images in clusters and images imbedded into crop circle pattern. They are still a mystery. This is one that is an exciting communication device, one that we are still learning about.

At first, the information was very general. Then it was established though that these images be called *signs* not *symbols*, the preferred terminology.

> *The symbols that have been given to you are a means of communicating the important messages and purposes in life. It is important that the main themes be transferred. Most of the information contained is also transferred by telepathy.*
>
> *Some of the symbols are used as a message to other spirits announcing that the sender has attained a specific level. Others are calls for*

> *help, used by all human beings at some time. However, when the meaning is understood then there is better communication. These symbols are for a specific purpose other than merely a connection to other planets and spirits.*
>
> *When they are placed in one direction with the arrowhead pointing down, they are asking for help from Earth spirits. When the arrow is facing up the Earth Beings are telling they are ready to communicate with the rest of the universe. It also indicates that they are in balance. When a spirit uses, or human uses a symbol that is not correct, it is not only miscommunication (which CAN be corrected through telepathy) but can bring trouble to the human or the planet if many are using symbols incorrectly. All symbols must be used with peace and love in mind.*
>
> *You will notice that some are symbols from other languages or other races. These peoples had partially learned what is important.*

This last sentence applies to the cultures that I referred to at the beginning of this section -- Tibetan, Chinese, Sanskrit, Japanese, Sumerian and Akkadian. These are ancient cultures, going back into a time when there was regular communication with the peoples of many planets. This relationship was seen as quite normal, not strange or fearful as some think today.

I had been receiving random signs for some months when I decided I wanted to know about the connection of the signs with some of my friends. Consequently, I went into a meditation and specifically asked for the relevant signs for these 13 people. Out of more than 20 signs, 14 signs were of some significance. Three more signs were identified for only me. One other person was given 3 signs and everyone else received two each. Initially, there seemed to be no pattern developing with these associations:

- Five signs were shared by two people each.
- Four were given to three groups of three.
- Four signs were given to four different individuals
- One sign was given to four people.

I immediately went into an analytic mindset trying to figure the connection to the signs. When I looked at the groups of people who received the same sign, there seemed to have no common theme. They are different ages, different genders, and even different astrological signs. Later, I received the following:

> *Each of these symbols represents the universal tribe that the people came from. Each powerful family in Egypt and other places of landing would have an obelisk in front of their home with the symbols. They were almost like addresses and family names. The pharaoh's home had two pillars with 6 symbols on each. The pharaohs were connected to the Earth and the universe. Other families were connected only to the universe.*

What is a universal tribe? At first look, many might speculate these are the astrological signs or the lost tribes of Israel. Are they associated with Mayan culture which understands the power of 13? Human conjecture can devise many answers to this question, none completely accurate. A universal tribe is connected to the concept of the individual essence.

An individual essence is the role or personality energy carried by each fragment, or soul essence in the TAO or *Tota*l. In this case, TAO has a different meaning from the YIN/YANG.

All universal tribes existing in all of the Universes have many essences. It is imperative that each tribe have a balanced blend of the roles for the effective order. This comes to six pairs of matching energies plus one individual energy for a total of thirteen (13) energies.

Whenever a group migrates or moves to a new location, a balanced mixture of essences, or specific energies should move in unison. Probably the easiest way to understand these 13 energies is through the Michael teachings.

While the teachings of the Michael entity have been around for eons, knowledge was isolated and little known. During the 1970s though, awareness grew and the understanding spread. The Michael entity consists of more than 1,000 essences or personalities, each very powerful. I'm sure other channeled entities spoke of the roles and personalities of individuals but Michael teachings are the most popular. Here is a simple overview.

When a soul leaves the TOTAL, or TAO, it is assigned a role which is carried from one lifetime to the next. This is how the soul approaches all lessons throughout its existence. While other aspects of the soul may change according to what is required at a particular time, the role remains constant.

To complicate things a little more, I was also given more information about this, which explains why it is often difficult to recognize a particular role in a person.

Printing this message will impress upon the reader that sometimes the roles are obvious and sometimes they are obscure. The energy of our souls has a delightful ability to flow in a form that feels safe and comfortable. After silently pondering roles and the Michael information, I was told:

> *You asked about the roles of souls. This is not given only to Michael. Rather, it is given to all creatures at the time of creation. We mean that all forms know of the roles and can respond as such. It is important to understand that in each orb, you can change role in appearance to accommodate other beings. This does not change the role of who you are, simply adopt the other role so that others will accept, much like a chameleon in your world. In our world, we do not need chameleons or shape-shifters, we must simply think change and it is so.*

There are seven roles identified within three categories, each with two roles and a third category with one role. The roles within a category are complimentary. Each one has general descriptive attributes, one positive, and one negative. The roles and these attributes are:

INSPIRATION ROLES:

Server/Slave – Service/Bondage
Priest -- Compassion/Zeal

EXPRESSION ROLES:

Artisan – Creation/Self-deception
Sage -- Expression/Verbosity

ACTION ROLES:

Warrior – Persuasion/Coercion
King -- Mastery/Tyranny

ASSIMILATION ROLE:

Scholar – Knowledge/Theory

To make up the 13 energies, there are two representatives of each role. That is 2 priests, 2 artisans, etc. The scholar role is one of adaptation. One of the traits of this role is to make up what is needed in the other 12.

When asked why there must be 13, why not just the 7, this is what I was told:

> *One cannot accomplish by itself. They need a backup to push the accomplishment. It is not enough to have the opposite, there needs to be a like-minded energy to push. Each person on your planet in human form can or should be able to recognize the catalyst for their tasks. Some call this a task-mate. This implies, however, sharing the work. We do not mean this. Rather, we mean that one supports the other and each does his or her own work.*

As physical beings emigrate or colonize various locations, there must be a multiple number of 13 for success of the project. For example, 7280(560 clusters x 13) or 585(13 x 45 clusters) are possible totals of those involved. This ensures that all skills, knowledge and connections are present. When we look at the positive and negative attributes, you can see why this is so. It also explains why so many today view a task-mate as someone who holds all the qualities not considered positive.

The entire compilation is known as the *Universal Tribe*. The universal tribe is simply a very large multiple of 13, almost infinite, containing all desired attributes needed for a successful community. We also need to remember that it is not necessary for a soul carrying a specific role to be physically present; it can be on the same planet and in telepathic communication with the gatherings.

As you can imagine, it is impossible to give the signs for each tribe but when an individual has an affinity for a particular sign, then it will invariably be a tribal symbol.

Note where this sign occurs in your life and note the time. Then note, what else is happening around the same time and location. Later, they get to use this tool to request more universal information.

Various signs refer to other cultures. Information mentioned that is linked in some way to a culture does not always imply that it came *directly* from that culture. Often the information coming through in meditations or a channeling will merely state: "This sign is from "*a particular*" culture and means …"

The initial signs were very basic, a straight line or a curve. As the number increased, they became more complex. Later I saw smaller signs that appeared to be attached or connected to a basic sign. This was very different from phrases where they were very separate and distinct. I later discovered that the addendums as I began calling them were just that, extensions of the original word.

For comparison we can look at current last names. Long ago, a man in a small village would be referred to by his first name or his trade, such as *Adam*. Over time, communities needed to differentiate between father and son so they added "son" to the name to indicate the "son of Adam". Hence, we have Adamson or Thomson.

This is the same principle with the signs. In the beginning, they made no sense. However, I guess as I became more accepting, somebody or some energy force felt they could give me more information. I must have moved from kindergarten to grade one! When a sign begins as a basic drawing, there will almost always be additions to it, providing additional meaning.

General Signs

I had almost two dozen signs in my repertoire before I received a phrase or sentence. I had a title for a book with no idea of the content. Possibly as a way of telling me that I was on the right track, they showed me two sentences to accompany the title, one each for WITHIN and BEYOND.

The first sentence translates into:

Sign #1 PEACE IS WITHIN

The next sentence translates into:

WITHIN & BEYOND: REVISITED

Sign #2: PEACE and LOVE from BEYOND

I was told the meaning of the last sign, without the details means "*Togethe*r"

"We can't go WITHIN without going BEYOND and we can't go BEYOND without going WITHIN. They go together"

Sign 3 TOGETHER

A short time ago, a valued friend, Hendrika Pudek, was shown following diagram in a dream. Later, she received an explanation. I found it particularly interesting because it was *Michael* entity that gave her the sign and spoke through her two days later. The information I included about the roles came at a different time and yet they complement each other.

#4 The Diagram as it was shown to Hendrika

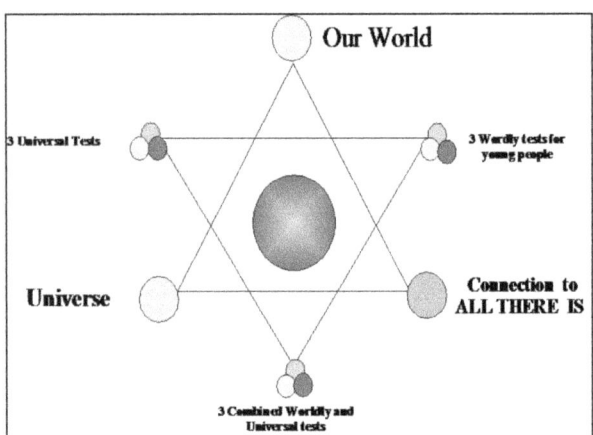

Well look at that, yellow light - World. You're born there, experience there and you learn there, what you call good and bad. Not all of you know by now. We want to tell you that 35% of human beings are still hanging on to the earth-plane as the only a learning planet. While 65% of all human beings are smarter; they think and open up and connect with the universe. One of the triangles on the diagram represents the Connection - Universe- Earth Plane.

Good, good, universe is where you learn more, 65% have reached out, looked and thought about the universe. Out of 65%, 40% looked beyond- further. They realized we are not alone and have more to connect with. They finally saw that there is much more to learn, to see and connect with. This is where, in between the universe and ALL THERE IS. You realized so many more planets and beings were there

to learn from, know about and connect with "All There Is". Only about 20% know and connect with "All There Is". It has taken many years to come that far. Work, give it all you have and see what is brought to you. Many where you are now, have visited planets, talked to those beings and have learned from them. Those young people that are coming, their lifetimes will be longer than yours. With their knowledge and determination, results will be much faster. On the diagram, they have 3 lights to connect with the Total. Green- Go! Yellow- Slow down, Red - Stop and think! But their stop will not be long, since their path is not like yours. No "S" and no threading back. They'll go straight ahead. They will bring all countries into balance first, and then work the balance with the connection to the Universe and all in a straight line to the Total.

I've already written about the importance of recognizing signs in your own world and there will be even more to come. This sign acknowledges the work that Hendrika has done. She was able to receive it, remember it and present it to us providing a good example of how we can use signs.

It is also relevant that the shape was a six-pointed star for two reasons.

First, it is the same as a 2 dimensional view of the MANU NYMBA, the minute particle of our being. This contains the Akashic records and the DNA of the Universe.

Second, it is a similar 2 dimension view of the MER-KA-VAH. This surrounds our body and is a vehicle for returning us to our higher state of consciousness.

While reviewing this drawing, I kept going back to the word "tests". Because of school conditioning, most people react to the word "test", preferring instead the word "checking" or similar word. I found I was reacting in a similar manner. These *tests* are nothing more than life lessons. One is learning patience, the second is learning to love and the last is learning to give it.

)
(

#5 Introduction

This is a simple sign and an appropriate introduction. Some time ago after receiving these, I traveled to the Hopi lands in Arizona. I noticed that I kept holding my cupped hands this way as I spoke to resident people. My left hand was on top and my right on the bottom. I queried and was told that this was an ancient Hopi greeting. When they depart, the hands are reversed, left on the bottom and right on the top. It also is a very important sign, indicating a closure to a meeting.

(
)

#6 Verbal farewells

Comparing this with verbal farewells, we see a connection. A few words such as "sayonara" indicate a permanent good-by.

Our sign equals this verbiage. Others such as 'so long' or "'til we meet again." refer to a temporary absence. When this is the situation, the palms are held face up, like a broad U.

#7

It is another way of saying:
"We will keep the energy flowing." Or
"We will keep the open communication and friendship alive."

I have also discovered this was part of the alphabet used by ancient cultures now extinct. It is the equivalent of our "H" in the English alphabet. It carried a sound of H as in *hope* and *healthy*. I find the word examples appropriate since when greeting someone, you have hopes of a successful friendship or connection. When departing, it there's a wish that the departing person stay healthy.

Originally, this sign came from an asteroid named **Nüsē**. Nüsē is in a universe far beyond ours. I was told that the Nüsēans were a small dark people with very dark hair. Although they were small, their form was perfect and very symmetrical. They carried this perfection into their communication. Most of their communication was telepathic, although they did have written language to communicate with other cultures.

As I was being shown these people, I was also hearing symphonic music. Through telepathy, they send this music, almost like a performer upon a stage. Other signs came to Earth from these people, but this was the most significant and the most lasting.

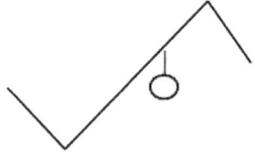

#8 - Transitions

This sign is a combination of cuneiforms and soft curves. It provides information about our past on Earth as well as data and messages from other planets and spirit guides.

Since it is multidirectional, we receive AND send information from both the universe and the Earth. Looking back into ancient history this makes sense. It is a transition sign, equivalent to a bat in Native American lore. It is also an initiation.

It is important to understand that whether you see this sign during meditation or begin to work consciously with it, you are keeping the core of which you are and simply adding to it. I like to think of it as an extension of your schooling.

Unlike butterflies and snakes that represent transformation, you can expect a total change, much like a new play on stage.

Sharing information with the Universe and the Earth opens many doors for the change that is bound to come. The image I was shown was:

> The two angled arms indicate that we need to pay attention to the past and prepare for the future while staying in the present. Since the "light bulb" hanging from the present is a soft curve, we can anticipate new information coming from our guides, wherever or whoever they may be. We must also watch for new signs from nature.

Cuneiform signs

Peoples of long ago accredited almost all early writing systems to divine sources. Cuneiform writing and signs are no exception. This style is one of the oldest, originating in the Middle East and Western Asia around 3,000 BCE. Cultures in these regions did not have ink or parchment paper so relied on scratching letters on wood, stone or coarse paper. Later on the Vikings adopted this style, using it well into the Middle Ages. Since these cultures are the forerunners of our western culture, it is not surprising that the signs given to me in the beginning were in that form.

My information stated that when this form of a sign appears, it is showing some form of Earth bound information. Some meanings were immediately apparent; others are not as simple. As you will later discover, these frequently became addendums to the soft curve signs, which I received later.

RUNES & the Alphabet

These images are not numbered the same as those coming from the spirit guides. These cuneiforms have been around a long time. The quantity in use at any time in history ranged from sixteen to twenty- four. From what I have been able to determine, the original quantity was 24, matching the Greek alphabet. Later the Danish sixteen- rune alphabet, called ***the futhork*** developed from this. The name FUTHORK was the name for the original first six letters.

Here is the sixteen-letter alphabet.

The Futhork Alphabet -16

The original 24 rune alphabet matched the Greek and Latin, making translation moderately easy.

"I" and "J" share the same rune. "U, V and W" also share the same rune.

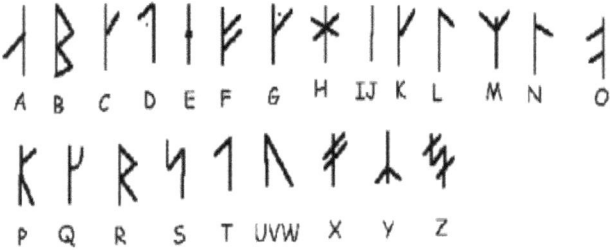

Original Rune Alphabet - 24

Just as there are variations within our culture and the Mayan culture, there are variations within the Viking culture world. The following are the Runes as they appeared in The Book of Runes.

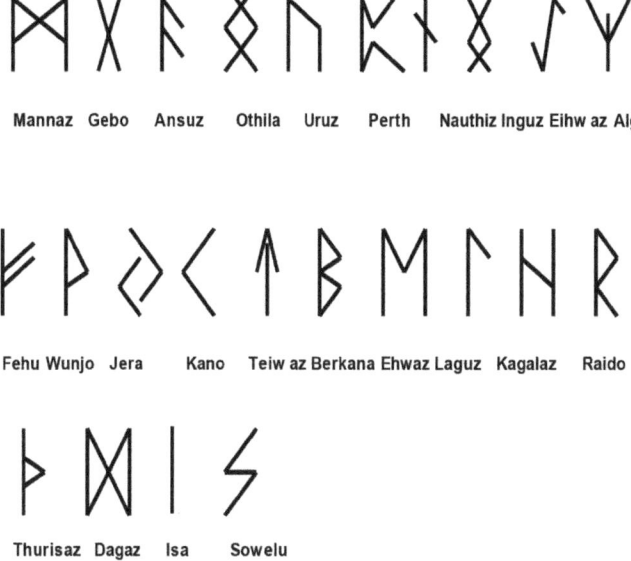

Signs 1-4 are important *general* signs that do not fit any specific category of signs. Signs 5-8 do. The Runes are cuneiform signs but since people around the world recognize them, they are not new; therefore, I have not given them a reference number.

Nevertheless, it is important for readers to match the rune images with information coming through their meditations. The following signs may resemble other images but the information came through after I began working with each sign.

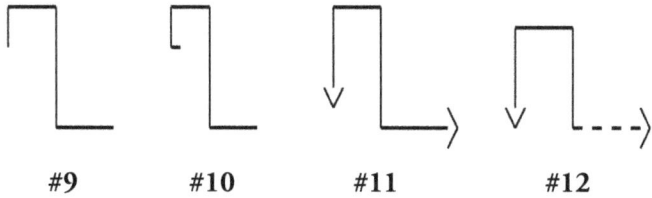

This is actually a series of signs. There are no addendums as I have defined. Rather they build on the previous, much like "C" evolving into "G", "o" becoming "b" or "d".

As I drew these signs inside my head, I became aware of two things.

- One was the *size* of each arm and the other was the importance of drawing direction.
- In all the signs, the vertical strokes MUST be drawn from top to bottom.
- The horizontal strokes MUST be drawn from left to right.
- In addition, the pen MUST be lifted at the end of each stroke; the image cannot be continuous.

In **#9**, the first arm had to be significantly shorter than each of the other three arms. When this sign is seen, it indicates limited information is coming through.

These four signs deal with evaluating your internal truth and learning to speak it, hence the arrows. With the small left arm, the receiver is living very much in the present with little knowledge of ancient understanding. Initially you look at a small detail and relate it to your surroundings. Next, you go deeper, seeking and receiving more details. You notice that the left arm gradually gets longer until it reaches **#11** and **#12** where more information rises to the surface from your human past.

In modern society, most see arrows as directional markers but we must remember that they also link us with our distant past. Arrowheads have been an archaeological finds for decades. Typically, they indicate a hunting/gathering culture, but there is more. Carrying an arrowhead gives the holder

WITHIN & BEYOND: REVISITED

strength and power. It also indicates that the person IS strong and powerful. Choosing to wear an arrowhead on a chain or string around our necks is a conscious action that increases our strength, power and connection. Here again the direction tells us the story. When the arrowhead is facing down, it is drawing from the universal energy. When it faces up, it is drawing energy from the earth.

It is important at this point to review the MANU NYMBA and its directions. Choosing an arrowhead on a chain will amplify the power of the MANU NYMBA. The arrowhead is the point of the two triangles. Holding an arrowhead in our hands as we do a MANU NYMBA meditation increases the intensity.

#13

#14

#15

#16

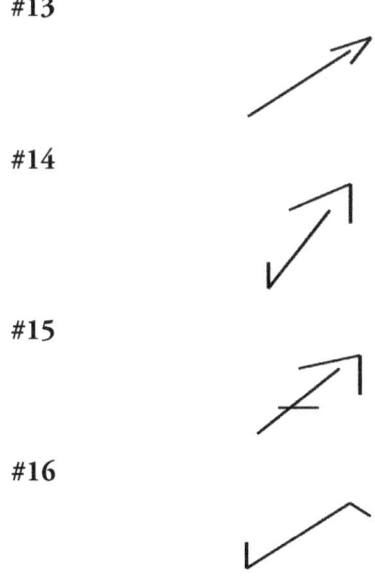

All these signs can be reversed, facing right or facing left. For convenience only the one direction is displayed. The main use of these signs was directional for migratory peoples. However, there is another use.

When a sign is used on an obelisk and one sign faces a specific direction, you can expect a similar sign farther down facing the opposite direction completing the circuit; much like a magnet's positive and negative poles. This simply states that whatever pictograph or sign is between them can be found at this location.

Putting it into modern terms, if it was a cattle ranch, then you would expect to see a pictograph of a cow on the obelisk.

#13 is a simple directional arrow. It indicates the strength and power flowing into the future. If the arrow or arrowhead is short or small, then the reader will know that pursuing that direction may not necessarily be profitable.

#14 has a grounding arm. This arm can also be angled, indicating a starting point. For example, slanted to the left, it tells the reader to go to the left and THEN move forward to get food or whatever. This is clearer than placing the two main arrows at an angle, inviting misinterpretation.

#15 is an invoking sign. This is commonly used in combinations because it strengthens the message of the other signs.

One of the uses for **#16** is informing future travelers or wanderers who has gone before. It is a potent sign carried by many people as they moved around the world; unfortunately eroded away over time.

There would have been a massive amount of information that would have been available to us if it had not been eroded. Instead, we had to wait for the recent research *proving* that the pygmies of Africa are connected to all races around the world

There is a large series of references on the internet under Pygmies & DNA. The original or ancient people (in this case, the pygmies) had a particular characteristic, gradually changing through interbreeding, climate and nutrition. If the signs had not been eradicated, we could retrace the steps as easily as a traveler of their time.

By varying the lengths and angles of the arms of **#16**, they told the direction travelled, how far away and where they were headed.

It would tell the reader that the potential harvest was vast regardless of type, food or energy. Unless it can be included in the sign, as at **#17**, then it is the sign immediately preceding that is affected. A comparison might be a quartz crystal enhancing the power of another stone such as a rose quartz.

However, when both a left and right directional arrows are placed together as in **#17**, it points to food or a resource. This can be anything from fuel to food or a rituals vortex. This calls for a combination of pictographs and the signs. The travelers would depict what could be expected if you traveled in that direction.

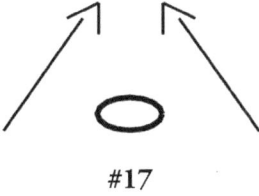

#17

Originally, there must have been a complex message attached to these signs that originated in the stars. The first alterations came about when humans chose written and spoken languages over telepathy. Initially, we have the individual interpretation, and then the adjustments that occurred as people wandered over the globe.

Most of us can relate to language and dialects. We can look first at the similarities between languages such as Japanese, Chinese and Korean or Russian and Greek. The lettering is slightly different in the two examples. Later within the same language, we discover original spellings staying constant but the pronunciation and meaning changing. As a Canadian, I have encountered Parisian French and Quebec French. Both started from an original root but the paths forked and we end up with two similar, yet different languages. Another strong example is the English language. We have Old English, Middle English, and Formal English. All readable by students of one another but it is difficult. So it is with signs. The drawing is the same but the meaning varies. I suspect this is why more information has not been forthcoming.

#18 is complex and a mystery. I received no information other than *pay attention.*

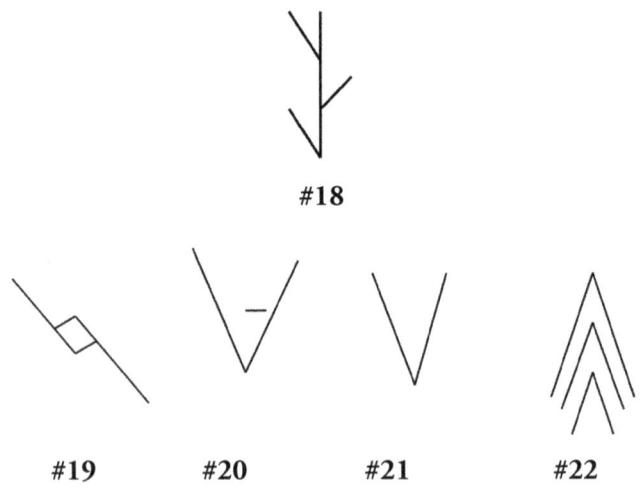

These signs differ from the previous set, as these are not directional but instead provide information.

#19 is one of the latest signs to come to me. It appeared as two checkmarks with a box joining the two arms. I may call it a lightning bolt but I must stress that it is NOT a vertical lightning bolt. It is on an angle for a reason. The left arm flows into the past, up and back. The right arm flows into the future, down and forward. The box is NOW, where we should live.

If we spend too much time either in the past, coping with regrets or in the future, worrying about what is yet to happen, it puts weight on the arms and the box and our living goes out of balance. When this happens, we are blocked from fulfilling our life tasks PLUS we are blocked from communicating and receiving the information we are meant to obtain.

So much of my channeled information emphasizes balance in our body and our lives that I was not surprised when this information came through. It is a valuable sign for us to know and recognize.

When we know what to look for, we can then discover when we are not in complete balance.

For readers who like to have tangible images of the signs, this is one is ideal. All that is needed is the two arms made out of a lightweight material and form a small box. Papier-mâché is a suitable medium; lightweight and will float as the arms shift. If the model is less than 4 inches, we can place it in our palm and hold it during a meditation.

#20 and **#21** are examples where additional information is added afterwards. Initially, all I saw was a large "V" sitting in a void. The "V" is the protective vehicle surrounding us as we work on our life tasks. Later the little line in the middle of the V (**#20**) appeared; it seemed to be floating. Before we can accomplish any task in our life, we must be balanced and centered.

This sign shows us the importance. If we imagine the "V" is filled with a liquid and the little line is floating, then we can visualize the line moving from side to side as the balance is thrown off. In our daily lives, this might happen when we spend too much time working, over exercising or socializing. All aspects of our life must be given the appropriate emphasis to maintain the balance. It is also the forerunner of the large "U" that we could open up to receive.

#21 indicates the additional information and support that is available to us when we are balanced. If we are not, then the little line on top of one or the other arm is thrown off and is displayed on the side like this.

#22 turned out to be an interesting sign. It can be read several ways. The answer is usually apparent when we stop to look at what is happening in our lives when the sign appears.

Firstly, it tells us that we need to work as a group, not alone. Many of us try to struggle to achieve in isolation when it is not necessary.

The second explanation is the trees and the forest. So often, we focus on a single tree and miss the beauty of the forest, or the reverse. Seeing this sign is an indication that we need to take a closer look. Are we spending too much time refining detail? Are we spending too much time looking at the overall result, ignoring details?

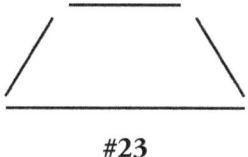

#23

This is an addendum sign. During the time of the obelisks construction, this was added to many signs. Usually it was placed underneath the other signs, telling others the name of who owned the obelisk, tent, property or whatever was displayed behind the obelisks. In this way, a person could identify the clan or family. If there were more than one clan or family living at that location, the sign was placed at the TOP, indicating ownership but not the sole resident.

Soft Curve Signs

Universal energy flows softly and smoothly, hence my choice for a sub-title. When we get a sense of fast moving energy presenting an image for us, it means two things...one the meaning of the sign and secondly the recipient is out of balance. Being out of balance limits our ability to pay attention and absorb information coming through. There are many ways to bring your identity into balance but linking the balance indicator to signs calls for specific action.

The easiest way is carrying healing stones. The three bodies, body, mind and spirit, require specific colors.

The body might need both healing and grounding stones. Red, orange and green stones, the colors of the lower chakras, are good for this purpose.

The mind, including emotional and mental activities needs stones for easing stress and sharpening the acuity.

Generally any stone that is blue or mauve is useful. However the following stones, while not all blue and mauve, are recognized as powerful for mental clarity: Emeralds, Malachite, Turquoise, and Lapis Lazuli.

For the spirit, the seventh chakra, deep purple amethyst, opal and ivory are helpful.

If carrying powerful stones is your chosen route, then I recommend that the reader consult a good quality gem book and make a selection. They do not have to be large and you may want several for each purpose. This gives you the opportunity to vary the daily selection for maximum effective.

Quite naturally, reducing your activities and meditating brings your body into balance.

The last way to bring about balance is through numbers. Carrying various quantities of specific objects, such as stones, is a great balancing tool. To determine the quantity required at any particular time, refer to the section on Numbers. As I said in that section, it is not recommended to jump back and forth searching for the easiest or best answer. However, if, after following one school for a while you feel another is better suited, then make a switch.

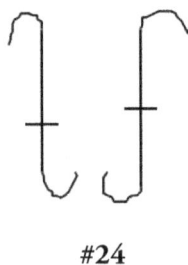

#24

This sign may appear to be a combination sign but the vertical bars are not part of the message; they are simply connectors. The upper curves, or cups, are cradles of life. There are two ways to look at these signs.

The first way usually shows up in meditations or nature images. It shows us what our general living style is at any particular time. If the bottom curves leads, looking like an "f" then we are spending most of the time in the physical world. Only the individual can decide if this is too much for a balanced being. If there are cross bars on the sign, this then tells us what other influences exist. If the top curve is on the left, then we are not spending sufficient time in the physical world and perhaps we need to look at what is going on in our life.

The second way of looking at these signs is a little more complex. It deals with life and death. This can be an actual death or birth of soul and body. It can also be a birth or death of a phase of living. Regardless, the down curves are protectors from the other worlds. When this sign showed up to a traveler, recorder or timekeeper, it was telling the observer that there has been a birth or death. When the curve is on the right, as in the first image, it is a birth, with the soul, moving from the spiritual life into physical life.

In the second image, the cradle is on the left, physical life. It tells the observer that the individual has left the current life (cradle of life) and moved on to a new world, receiving protection (the down cradle). Remember that the flow is from top to bottom, from left to right. An easier way to think of the cradle holding something in my hands and the downward curve was someone watching over.

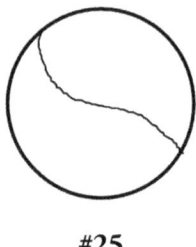

#25

At first glance, this looks like the Yin-Yang symbol but it is not.

When we look at the Yin-Yang symbol below, we see that it is divided vertically into two halves with small circles of the opposing colors in each half. **#25** divides into two parts at an angle, not a vertical division. However, there is sufficient similarity to realize that they probably had a mutual origin.

While exploring my interest in Eastern philosophies some time ago, I learned that when the Chinese mapped out the cycle of sun, they created a drawing looking very much like #25, the Yin/Yang symbol and the Nautilus shells.

Below is a graphic illustration of the sun's cycle. Using a vertical pole, they watched the sun's shadow as it waxes and wanes. The image reminds us of the Yin/Yang. The nautilus shell is also visible.

#25 is identifiable, although a little tipped to the left.

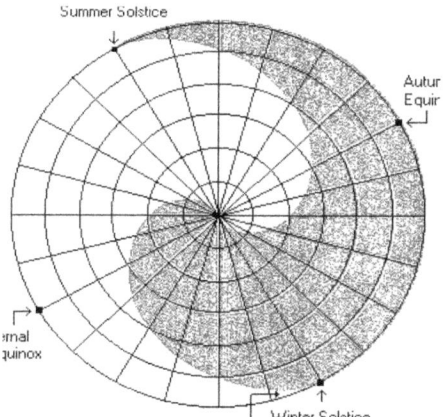

Take a look at these images and see if you agree. Both the Yin/Yang and the nautilus shell represent balance and harmony. Consequently, when **#25** appeared to me, it only made sense that it was simply a version of the other two images. To my surprise, it meant more than that.

Yes, it does mean balance but the fact that the line flows from the imaginary times of 10 o'clock and 4 o'clock telling us:

- The traveler is on the right path.
- It is a good place to rest.
- There is plenty of fuel.
- Food is nearby.

If the line flowed from *any* other position on the circle, one of the three would be in short supply. There would still be balance since four messages are valid; it simply means that there is a little more work to achieve one of the four goals.

Possible interpretations could be: there is fuel but it is farther afield or has to be chopped or the food is of limited variety. Regardless of the additional information, there is still peace and harmony coming with this sign. It simply requires further exploration.

#26

This sign seems to be a basic building curve for universal signs. This is not surprising since it is relatively simple to draw. When the arch flows from left to right, it refers to information linking past and present. When it sits vertically, the sign will be almost entirely universal knowledge. The degrees of slant indicate the amount of universal influence. This is one sign that almost requires addendums.

#27

This is quite an exciting sign for me. While taking a long walk one day I noticed the clouds in this formation. By itself, this is not unusual but they stayed in this formation for more than 10 minutes, other clouds in the sky continued flowing back and forth. I was then given a message:

"Forget the past, move into the future."

WITHIN & BEYOND: REVISITED

I reflected on what was happening in my life at that particular time and this made sense.

It was one more confirmation that signs give us information from the universe or from the Earth's past. They are either very general or very specific to a person.

The next three illustrations making up **#28** require accuracy in the making.

The **Curves** themselves refer to **time**.

The **Dots** are just that – a point in time. When the curve is facing up, it is time to come. The curve facing down is time past. The circle refers to an event.

In all three examples where the dot is placed indicates how soon. If it is to the left, then the time is imminent. To the right, it is a ways away.

#28

The Alphabet

The alphabet letters shown to me are only a small segment of what emerged as peoples wandered the Earth, the Runes being one example and the Sumerian alphabet another. I have not been shown many letters but what was given illustrates the diversity and potential for further information and surprises. I also saw the universal influence on the letters. The letters use all three forms –cuneiform, soft-curve and combination.

There is one trait that seems to have survived the millenniums and migration of people is the importance of the direction. We don't see that often today but it is seen in formal, artistic writing.

When writing Chinese characters with ink and brush, then direction determines the amount of ink or paint at each spot. Earlier in the book, I wrote: *In all the signs, the vertical strokes MUST be drawn from top to bottom. The horizontal strokes MUST be drawn from left to right. In addition, the pen MUST be lifted at the end of each stroke; the image cannot be continuous.* These rules apply to the alphabet letters presented here.

Some time ago, I received these signs along with its information.

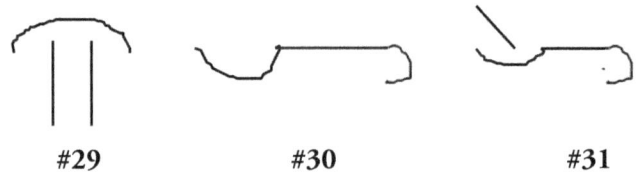

#29 **#30** **#31**

These are the basis of all alphabets. Generally they are combination signs allowing for greater flexibility.

#29 can appear with one or two vertical pillars.

#30 is written in many directions, vertical, upside down, left-right and right to left.

#31 is the same as **#30**, with the addition of the addendum line flowing out of the 'cup'.

There can be many lines and again these lines can face many directions, up, down, 45° and parallel.

I must remind the reader that when we say "all alphabets", we are referring to what was here many eons ago, not our current cultural languages.

This next set of signs relate to the English alphabet. As I pondered the information, I realized that the shapes reflected the use of our muscles around our mouth and face.

WITHIN & BEYOND: REVISITED

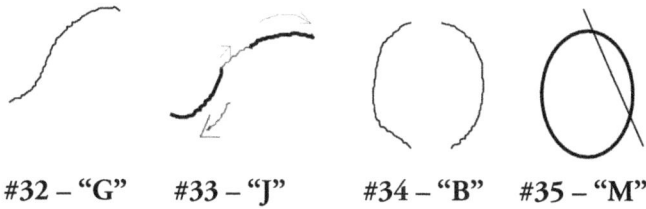

#32 – "G"   #33 – "J"   #34 – "B"   #35 – "M"

While I hoped for all the signs that match the letters of our alphabet, it was not to be. These do however give us good examples of how the system works.

The first two *alphabet* signs that I received were **#32** and **#33**. The sounds were very clear.

#32 was "G" as in "GAY" and

#33 was "J" as in "JAY".

Of course, I queried with a human mind. I asked, "If the "G" is a hard "G", then why is that sign not darkened? My logic said that a soft sound, the "J", should be written lightly.

Here is the explanation – The sign is darkened, not for the sound that comes out but rather the amount of facial muscle movement required to make the sound. I then went on to study my face as I made these sounds.

A "G" (**#32**) requires little movement. The sound can be made by the tongue and air alone. This sign is drawn in a continuous, fluid line from the bottom to the top.

A "J" (#33) requires a relaxed jaw, calling for the facial muscles to move through relaxation, hence the darkening of the curves. The creation of this sign is very specific. The lower curve is drawn from the top to the bottom, thickening it as it reached the end. Next the center piece is drawn from the bottom up. Finally the top curve is drawn from the center to the top, thickening the line as it reaches the top.

#34 is the sign for the letter "B", again is very logical. The two halves of the circle *cannot* touch. They are apart for two reasons. Firstly, after uttering the sound, the lips are apart. I'm sure that the second reason came after. The two loops on the letter "B" equal the open lips. Both these curves are drawn from the top to the bottom.

The last *alphabet* sign shown was the letter "M", **#35**. To make the "m" sound, the lips are closed and air is pushed into the mouth, making a vibration sound. The line through the top of the circle is off center to differentiate it from other signs and to stress the flow- through of air.

This sign has two purposes, --

- Letter of the alphabet
- Information.

For unknown reasoning, the sign **#36** equals the letter "L" as well as meaning "Don't stay, move on."

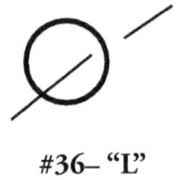

#36– "L"

Combination Signs

There are a number of signs including information from the universe – soft curves, as well as information from the Earth's history – cuneiforms. In the previous section there were a few signs that, at first glance, might be considered combinations since they contained both straight lines and curves. However, the information obtained was only coming from the curves, NOT the straight lines. The lines' purposes were supportive or connectors only.

In this section each sign includes information from both sources.

The next sign has become one of my favorites. #37 came rather early in what I call *The Sign era*, a surprising departure from the basic, simple ones I had been receiving up until that time.

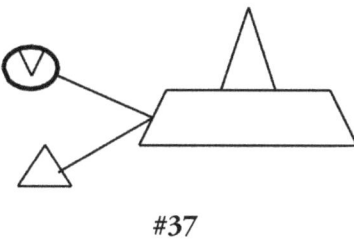

#37

This sign shows that the body is in balance. The little boat unfortunately does not mean there is any travel in the near future! However, it *does* mean that there is transportation *assistance* ahead. Depending upon the location and the time in history, this could mean anything from boats, repairs to airplanes.

The V within the circle is a symbol that when worn on the body bringing healing into the body. It represents magnetic energy. Placing the image where the healing is needed focuses the energy.

The triangle directs the universal energy into the body and into the Earth. How far apart these two images are tells us the level of seriousness; close together means things are not too bad. When the triangle is in conjunction with other images, it becomes a good grounding sign.

#38

I have included two cuneiforms signs, **#38**, here for direct comparison; both healing signs. When I first saw them, they were on two doors, separated only by a person standing. The one on the left, looking like an "M", brings healing into the throat and third eye of the person. The one on the right heals the heart.

It is important when working with either sign to place the patient in the proper position. For example, for the left sign the person would stand looking in a mirror. The practitioner would place hands on the throat first and secondly on the third eye.

For the heart healing, the person is in a prone position. As practitioner, you place your hands over the heart and the energy flows from your hands to the heart.

The two parallel lines represent the energy running from your hands.

Generally, the person in need of the healing will see the signs. A practitioner generally sees the sign when the client in question is present.

#39 -- Pathway to help

I saw the one on the left about two weeks before the second one appeared. My first reaction when I saw this was a gas gauge on a car. Since there is no such thing as a tangible fuel in the universe, it had to be something else. I received two answers.

1. The small center circle lets us know that we are on the right track, or path. The two arms forming the "V" guide us toward additional help. The one on the left guides to spirit help and the right hand one guides to more physical earth- bound help.
2. If these were on a road on Earth, then the one on the left informs us to keep going in the same direction, help or assistance is straight ahead. The other lets travelers know that they are leaving an area where assistance was available.

From the point where they are seen, individuals are on their own.

If these appeared in a dream or meditation, then we need to either look to our universal guides for information or search below. Searching below can make use of anything from that which is living on the planet, to aspects of the planet itself such as crystals, or water.

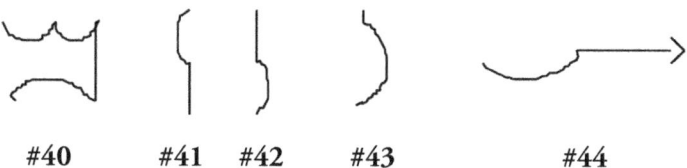

#40   #41 #42 #43   #44

There are many signs used as landmarks in our past just as there are today around the world. These are some of the images shown to me. As before, they can be multi-purpose.

#40 or the reverse is images that a traveler would see. However, this time it is not intended for the stranger. Most cultures hold their ceremonial sites as sacred and would not allow strangers to visit.

Since this sign could be used to indicate a village and clusters of houses as well as village and sacred sites, the stranger wouldn't know the difference.

The image #40 is written in one of the four directions. The two curves indicate a village while the one large curve indicates a ceremonial center. Again, these can be reversed.

For those familiar with the Maya world of the Yucatan peninsula in Mexico could envision this sign on the road between Chichen Itza and one of the smaller canters or villages. The large curve would refer to Chichen Itza. That the road leads to the left or right would show up on the vertical arm.

The arrow on **#44** indicates the importance of spiritual site and influence. The size of the curve and the distance of the arrow tell just how strong the influence is and how far away it is from the current position.

The next sign **#45** is a marker of a sacred school, teaching the young and honoring the old. While the inhabitants of local villages will know of its location, by erecting this sign, the village is telling strangers that they revere their elders and prepare their young. Education has never been random.

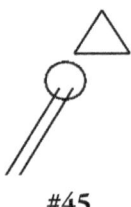

#45

Peoples around the world knew the importance of teaching their young; this was the key to their survival. This may have been routine functions as hunting for food, creating everyday clothing or preparing food.

In this first instance – hunting - it was probably a father, elder brother or uncle who took on this task. For everyday clothing, it may have been the mother or grandmother. However for ceremonial garments involving rituals and blessings, this likely fell to the elders or shamans of the village or community.

In addition, every village or society needed a healer, someone knowledgeable of herbs and plant life. Initially, the teachings were simple but as societies became complex, so did the teaching. They needed structured, sacred teaching.

Over time, people are becoming interested in native cultures but struggle to recapture lost knowledge and traditions.

While in Mexico studying the Maya, I realized just how important that ancient teachings had become. Had they not passed their wisdom from shaman or elder to younger generations, their culture would have been lost during the time of the Spanish invasions.

As archeologists or anthropologists wander through ancient ruins, it is difficult to find evidence of formal teaching practices, unless there is a system of writing.

While I did not see this specific sign on one of my trips to ancient Hopi ruins in Arizona, I did see the ruins of an ancient village in the Wupatki National Monument that followed the traditions. My spiritual information is that **#46** is a marker of a sacred school, teaching the young and honoring the old.

#46

This sign can be very comforting, indicating safety. This can be a safe haven for a family unit. It can also mean lodging of some type.

This is an excellent example of a need for a family addendum, or insignia. This image would probably go at the base of the sign.

A sign for safety and comfort is probably the most appropriate closing to the individual signs and the meanings.

Summary of the Signs and Their Meanings

This summary offers a quick reference which provides a confirmation of one definition for each reader. The information was channeled from pertinent spirit guides and you will be instructed by *your* guides as to what you need to pay attention to.

I'm sure some readers, based on their own experience, will question some of these meanings and I encourage this. Today, languages and cultures provide different approaches and interpretations, so it is with the signs. Not all of us lived at the same time or in the same regions so the signs evolved with a different interpretation for us. Here are the definitions relevant to my experience.

WITHIN & BEYOND: REVISITED

- **#1** -- Peace Is Within
- **#2** -- Peace from Beyond
- **#3** -- Together
- **#4** -- The Diagram as it was shown to Hendrika
- **#5** -- Introduction, Hello or Greeting
- **#6** -- Farewell
- **#7** -- Temporary parting
- **#8** -- Transition
- **#9** – Limited information coming
- **#10** – Living in the present
- **#11** – Information *from* the past
- **#12** -- Information *from* the past, indicating distance into time
- **#13** – Strength and power flowing into the future
- **#14** – Grounding arm and directional source
- **#15** – Invoking sign
- **#16** – Tells us who has gone down a path before
- **#17** -- Potential harvest
- **#18** – Unknown
- **#19** --Live in the Now
- **#20** – Add'l information is available, Recipient must be centered
- **#21** – Basic Curve linking earth and universal information
- **#22** – Work as a group
- **#23** – Family or clan identity addendum
- **#24** – Cradles of life, death or birth of phase of life
- **#25** – Traveler on the right path, food and fuel near
- **#26** – Past and Present
- **#27** – Forget the past & move into the future
- **#28** – Circle of events and time occurrence
- **#29** – Alphabet basics

- **#30** -- Alphabet basics
- **#31** – Alphabet basics
- **#32** –Letter "G"
- **#33** – Letter "J"
- **#34** -- Letter "B"
- **#35** -- Letter "M"
- **#36** – Letter "L" or don't stay, move on
- **#37** -- Body in balance but segmented
- **#38** --Healing signs
- **#39** -- Pathway to help
- **#40** --Village and ceremonial center
- **#41** -- Alternative sign to #40
- **#42** -- Shows size of center and distance as in #40
- **#43** -- Alternative sign to #42
- **#44** -- Importance of sacred site, influence on daily life
- **#45** -- Sacred school
- **#46** -- Safe Haven

TRAVELS, TALES AND TRUTHS OF THE CRYSTAL SKULLS

The previous two sections spoke of places where sacred information is located.

The **MANU NYMBA** is the smallest component of any physical being, yet it has been programmed with the most information – information for the single being *plus* the key to all relevant universal information. This information comes as part of our creation. Since it is the only source of personal coding, such as DNA, it goes to the top of the triangle, the pinnacle.

The **SACRED TREES** contain the details, not just the key, for the universe and society; gifted by the Lemurians.

The **CRYSTAL SKULLS** contain knowledge for all of creation throughout the cosmos. They came from the other worlds through Lemuria and other ancient worlds. Their energy is pure, powerful and mysterious.

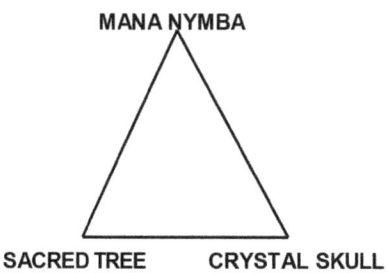

Because most of the known Crystal Skulls come from Central America and because we live in the Western world, there is a tendency to assume this is the only source location.

However, indigenes around the globe are aware of them through their legends and sagas; all Skulls are linked to native, original peoples. They have also been found in Peru, Russia, Tibet, China and naturally North America.

If I had not done any research and someone asked me "Who else knows about the skulls?" I would immediately think of the Hopi people.

Perhaps it is because I had a meditation some time ago where the Dalai Lama gave an ancient sacred skull to the Hopi for safe keeping. Or perhaps it is because the Hopi honor and live by the information and instruction they receive. When I visited the Hopi Mesas a few years ago, I was overwhelmed by their sense of integrity and honor. This prompted my study of their culture.

One of the Hopi stories passed down through generations is the story of The Emergence; a prophetic consequence that gives a lesson reaching far beyond the Hopi world. It is a lesson for all of humanity.

This lesson was summarized in the ***Hopi Shrine of the Covenant*** by *Tomas Mails and Dan Evehema* published by Marlow & Company.

On page 49, we find:

> *Those gifted with the knowledge of the sacred instructions will then live very cautiously, for they will remember and have faith in these instructions, and it will be on their shoulders that the fate of the world will rest.*

This quote does not specify the Crystal Skulls but it is so relevant. Today, there are many people, including the "Caretakers of the Skulls" who work with the skulls. In a sense they have the fate of the world upon their shoulders. Simply by working with skull energy, they balance the Sacred Tree energy producing the base of a pyramid which carries information for the Earth, our collective well-being and the Universe.

Perhaps unwittingly, but whenever a person works with a fragment of the total energy, he or she tacitly enters into a contract, or agreement, to support and teach all entities. This, then, must be followed very cautiously. Some readers may wonder what the fuss is all about; they have no contact with sacred trees or Crystal Skulls.

However, while we could exist without the pyramid base a person would have difficulty functioning. We can live in isolation with only the MANU NYMBA within us but it would be difficult.

We are social animals and to exist as compassionate, loving beings, we need information about our social structure and the universe in general. Therefore, we must acknowledge the interaction of what surrounds us and what preceded our current lives. This comes from the pyramid of information as shown:

Few people on this Earth Plane can understand and access all three sources. Anyone who has this ability is faced with the challenge of disseminating the wisdom without abusing personal power or ego.

Like the Hopi prophecy, they must live *very* cautiously, knowing their actions contribute to the fate of the world. For those who are not aware of their own ability, they must study, learn and understand as much as possible, hoping to make a difference as they share the discoveries. Neither one has an easy task.

When you read further, you will discover that Crystal Skulls and their wisdom are becoming more prevalent. This can be good or bad because as soon as someone is introduced to the skulls, their lives change. It can be bad because of the amount of responsibility falling on each person. The new responsibilities, knowledge and abilities touch everybody, there is no turning back.

THE TRAVELS

Crystal Skulls are exciting and mesmerizing. However, before I go into details about skulls, I need to share some of the information that came to me through many meditations. It begins with the Lemuria and Mayan culture.

The Lemurias created seeds for the Sacred Trees and stored the wisdom of their beliefs in Crystal Skulls. These skulls were programmed for three purposes <u>communication,</u> <u>knowledge</u> and <u>healing;</u> all necessary for a continuance of their lifestyle. Each tribe or group assigned one person to be the caretaker or scribe for their skull. This may have been a shaman, chief or medicine worker, depending upon the social structure of the people. Their mission was to verbally record the information and the key in songs and stories that could be passed down through generations. Later you will see just how vital this task becomes.

As we said before, there is a tendency in the Western world to confine the Crystal Skulls to Central America. However, skulls have been reported in Tibet, Africa, Europe, Peru and, Russia.

When the time came to leave their homeland, the Lemuria people traveled in four directions. While scientists have studied possible migration routes (see previous section), they depended upon physical proof but this does not always go back far enough in time.

Perhaps today's studies and research on Atlantis will produce some evidence. It will not provide solid information about Lemuria which is much older than Atlantis, but it could open the door to recognition. We know the Lemuria citizens traveled and seeded the Earth; we just don't have the details.

Legends and sagas throughout Central American confirm that the majority of the Lemuria people traveled to and settled in Central and South America, thus becoming the ancestors of the Maya. Their first settlements would have been on the Pacific Coast, later moving inland toward the regions where we find ruins today.

Although weather patterns varied somewhat over the millenniums, we can be fairly confident that the Pacific Coast region maintained the thick vegetation. Because of this, most ruins in this area are heavily overgrown and difficult to uncover.

Despite this, one skull surfaced in this area. It was unearthed by a professor of parapsychology, Nick Nocerino

This message from **SHA NA RA** was printed on a website: http://shanaracrystalskull.com

The message is as follows:

> *I am a child of the Earth, harvested, carved and used by humankind. In this time and in this place, I am a Shaman's tool of the highest order. My past is rich with the knowledge of the ages but I am not a God. I function only in conjunction with human energy and act as a facilitator of communication between the worlds within each individual. As such, I carry the collective knowledge and experience of everyone that has touched me. This collective energy is what gives me the potential of imparting Universal Love.*

> *In reality, I am but a mirror, a reflector of what is inside the heart of each individual. The only magic I possess is what I mirror from you. Whatever you see in my eyes is what you truly are. I can show you the depth, breadth and height of your own soul if that is what you need to see. I can break through the resistance of your mind and open doors to knowledge long forgotten. In this way I encourage personal growth and healing on every level.*
>
> *My message is one of unconditional acceptance. Just as there are many paths up the mountain, each individual has a unique way of walking their path. As a Shaman's tool, I illuminate the path of the individual as it relates to the journey of us all.*

Even though Nick Nocerino kept the exact location where he found his skull a secret, he did admit that it was in Guerrero state of Mexico, on the West Coast just south of Acapulco.

After the West Coast settlement, we know that the Maya moved into the midlands of Central America and the East Coast. We also know that it is extremely unusual for a group of people to stay in one location without expanding their territory. This happened here. Regardless of geographical changes to the Earth's surface, we are still able to develop a migratory path or trail for these people. Since they had come from the West, this leaves three directions for the Maya to take the Crystal Skulls.

Traveling north into North America makes it conceivable that the Maya and Lemuria nations were potential predecessors of the Hopi nation and other indigenes. In addition, there are similarities between the sacred teachings of both the Hopi and the Maya supporting this theory.

Traveling south in South America connects the Inca; definitely a cultural connection. Crystal Skulls have also been reported in Peru.

The last direction, east, is the one we will concentrate on here. It requires ocean travel, assuming of course it was not all land. The Lemuria residents found it relatively easy to travel from Lemuria in the Pacific Ocean in their ships. The ship was long and low with the stern end rising high above the water allowing for decorative design. Ocean navigation knowledge stays with a people; it is seldom lost.

Since most literature is seldom gathered in the order of publication, this is no exception. This book conforms to this premise.

When I found the information from the Cherokee medicine man, Harley Swift Deer, I was intrigued. In the teachings of his elders, they speak of four civilizations – Lemuria, Mu, Mieyhun and Atlantis.

I had not heard of Mieyhun, so the search began.

I discovered the Mieyhun people lived in Africa around the same time, or shortly after the time, of the Maya in Central America. When you verbalize the name, it sounds very similar to *Maya*.

Ignoring the other directions, let us look at this small faction of the Maya culture in Central America set sail and traveled to Africa to set up a new world.

Earlier, I mentioned that one person in each gathering was chosen to learn the keys and information stored within the crystal skulls. They could then guide the teachings of the skulls, securing the knowledge of the Lemuria people.

Often individuals or groups did not accept the teachings of the shaman or spokesperson for their gathering. When the Mieyhun settled in Africa, I believe the motivation was a desire to follow their personal beliefs without conflict.

A desire for the freedom to interpret their beliefs their own way is always strong. Looking back through history there are many examples of small groups breaking away from a larger assembly.

We can never say these interpretations are wrong. Each way is right for those who use it; it is the ego of the leaders causing problems. Break-a-way examples include Protestant vs. Evangelical vs. Catholicism, Orthodox Judaism or Conservative Judaism. These are large divisions but there are also many smaller groups such as the Quakers and Amish who believe their interpretation is correct. Explaining recent history such as these examples is moderately easy; it is the ancient history that is the problem.

Until we find ruins with some recorded documentation, we will never know for sure when and where segments of a culture traveled.

Regardless, I have been assured that my information is true. Scientists might disagree, arguing that there is no evidence. Their main type of proof used is matching the physical structure of inhabitants. Unfortunately, we cannot depend on the physiology of individuals to give evidence. Every culture has intermarriage, some stronger than others. Therefore, the only things that we can use as a benchmark are pyramids and the crystal skulls. The inclusion of pyramids will become apparent as you read further. So, let's look at pyramids first.

As the Lemuria or Maya residents traveled around the world, they built pyramids. We discover pyramids in almost every corner and country of the world: North America,

Central America, South America, Africa, Europe, India, Asia and perhaps the Antarctic continents.

Historians and archaeologists search for answers to these questions: "Where did they come from?" and "Who built them?" They had a mystery on their hands and they had to make a choice. The sites could be unearthed inviting looters before studying the site, or they could remain hidden beneath heavy forests and never disclose their message to us. Fortunately, in almost every location we can find ruins fitting the first category. Thanks to the commonalities amongst the explored ruins, we are able, despite looting and overgrowth, to discover the message or the key to it.

While it was not always the primary purpose of the pyramids, many had burial chambers within, allowing the departed leaders to be closer to the Gods. Some had mummified bodies such as the Egypt pyramids and the Shensi pyramids in China.

What we need to understand is that when a group breaks away, they amend the interpretations of the teachings. At first it is only a modest deviation, then gradually becomes bigger. So, as groups moved around the globe, their beliefs shifted. In Central America, it was the soul, not the body that was important. Later descendants in Africa and elsewhere believed the soul needed a body in the next life, thus mummification was born.

The pyramid shape allows the priests and shamans to move up away from the Earth energy giving clearer communication with their Gods. Regardless of the culture, there was always a place to stand at the peak. It might be small like the Egyptian's pinnacle or larger like the Mayan's flat platform.

Nevertheless, the peaks of all pyramids are designed to hold a specific Crystal Skull, the skull of communication. This Crystal Skull is the group's largest and purest crystal. Further down the sides would be places for other Crystal Skulls. Depending upon the directional side (N, S, E, and W) and the importance of the pyramid, the meaning varied.

Generally, though, the skulls that resided on the sides of the pyramids held only a fragment of the knowledge. Their function was to pass on relevant knowledge and healing to the masses. Crystal skulls that have been discovered today demonstrate this.

Some of the skulls, such as MAX, are healing skulls. Others like SHA NA RA were transmitters of knowledge, including healing.

In ancient times when the skulls resided at the pyramids, there was one person chosen to be a scribe, usually a priest or shaman. He was the only person who could be near the main Crystal Skull. He received and interpreted all the information coming through the skull.

This information would then flow down to the others on the path to the base. It has been said that it is important to bring skulls together of the same color or hue. This brings the fragments together, like a jigsaw puzzle. Since mankind cannot yet comprehend all the wisdom at once, the *Master* skulls remain hidden. This does not minimize the value of those surfacing, they carry valuable information but it is only a fragment.

Eventually, all the Crystal Skulls will be returning to the Maya of Central America, revealing far more wisdom and healing powers than we can possibly imagine today. This is what the Pleiades were referring to when they spoke through Barbara Marciniak in July, 2001. They knew that humans could not handle the power of the mass energy.

The Mayan Prophecy knows the power of the Crystal Skulls as well as the fragmented energies. This prophecy states:

> *"When the crystal skulls return to the sacred Mayan lands, the cycle of time for the returning of the Mayan cosmic consciousness will be set up as completed."*

Today, the work to bring the skulls back together is just beginning.

While I was in Mexico participating in one of the first of these gatherings, I was very aware of the power and the challenge facing the leaders, they have a formidable task. It is not simply calling the skulls home. The leaders must heal those who come to work with the skulls, balance the energy, and inform the public officials of the purpose and safety.

While the main Crystal Skulls will return to Central America, it is important to remember that as groups brake away from their 'mother' group, travelling the world, building temples and pyramids, they follow their interpretation of the knowledge provided by crystal skulls. Regardless of the various perceptions, it was still the Crystal Skulls that gave each group their wisdom. Every temple and pyramid around the world needs to have a Crystal Skull return home. These skulls will always return. This can be an intriguing idea when you think of a pyramid buried below 2,000 years of vegetation. Megaliths around the world are also connected. They come from a different branch of Lemuria and have a different purpose but the principle is the same. There were many tools used by the original people.

THE TALES

North American Teaching

One source tells us that skull power and knowledge went beyond the Central American and North American native cultures. According to a Cherokee Medicine man, Harley SwiftDeer, the skulls are part of a global history that has been kept secret until recently. It is now being revealed.

At the time when Chris Morton and Ceri Thomas were writing their book *The Mystery of the Crystal Skulls* published by Bear & Company, they interviewed Harley. He then told them the story of the Twisted Hairs.

He tells us that the Twisted Hairs are peoples from Central, North and South America who have passed on stories about the beginnings of life.

According to this, the beginning of life on Earth came from 12 planets. Each planet had specific information and skills. This information was stored in the crystal skulls and would become apparent when the time was right. The story continues:

> 'The elders of the Twisted Hairs say that in the very beginning there were 12 worlds with human life. These are planets that revolve around different suns and the elders met on a planet called Osiriaconwiya. This is actually the fourth planet out from the Dog Star, Sirius. It has two suns and two moons. They met here to discuss the plight of the planet of the children- and this is where we are today. This is Grandmother Earth. It is called Eheytoma in

our language, but it also represents 'the planet of the children" because it is the least evolved of all those planets with human life. So we are really one of a family of 12 planets.

Each of the other planets took the sum total of all knowledge and they encoded this knowledge into what can best be described, in modern-day terms, as a sort of holographic image computer called a crystal skull. These are absolutely flawless, perfect crystal skulls. These skulls have moving jaws just like our skulls so they were referred to as 'the singing skulls' and the entire configuration was known as 'the Ark of Osiriaconwiya'. Each skull represents a different planet's knowledge. The best way to think of it is we have computers today that have huge amounts of data stored which can be accessed. All of the crystal skulls store huge amounts of information, and they can be accessed if you understand how to do so.

Anyway, our cosmic elders took the Ark and encoded all of the knowledge of the 12 worlds with human life, which are called the 'sacred 12" planets or "grandmothers', and then they brought them here and they began to work with them and to teach the children of Grandmother Earth. These cosmic elders found a way to be able to move back and forth in their communications with the "Two-legged" here on Grandmother Earth.

And this really was a most impressive and valuable gift that was given to the children of this Earth, for it was the gift of knowledge. It was the greatest gift, for it was the root from which all could develop, it was the foundation from which we all could flourish.

And this is what originally happened and there was a period of great advancement. The elders from the other planets educated the children of this Earth and they gave them what are called 'the teachings of the sacred shields'.

The elders found a way to be able to communicate with the people of this Earth from their own planets, with the assistance of two great domes, one red and the other blue, that were located beneath the ocean. And they helped the people of the Earth to build four great civilizations, the civilizations of Lemuria, Mu, Mieyhun and Atlantis. And they used the knowledge of the skulls to begin the great mystery schools, the arcane wisdom schools, and the secret medicine societies. And they began to disseminate this information. The information arrived approximately 750,000 years ago and it began to be distributed on Grandmother Earth around 250 to 300,000 years ago. To help with the teachings other skulls were created here on Earth, but though life-size, their jaws do not move. There are many more of these skulls and they are known as the 'talking skulls', to separate them from the 'singing skulls' of the major Ark, which represents all of the knowledge of all of the 12 worlds as well as our own.

Maya Teachings

When the Spanish arrived in Central America, they banned all native practices. Like the Native American storytellers, the Mayan people knew they must preserve their teachings; they could not be lost. Therefore, an elder, or 'daykeeper' in each village became responsible for learning and keeping their wisdom secret, passing it down through generations.

Hunbatz Men is one of this generation's priest, elders or 'daykeepers'. Like Harley, he believes it is now time to share the wisdom for the benefit of the Maya and all living on our globe. Through Mystery School conferences and Mayan Workshops, Hunbatz is now sharing his knowledge. P.S. *I was honored to study with him.*

Throughout his writings and workshops in the Yucatan, Mexico, I frequently heard him repeat the Mayan prophecy: **"*When the crystal skulls return to the sacred Mayan lands, the cycle of time for the returning of the Mayan cosmic consciousness will be set up as completed.*"**

All a person needs to do today is travel through the ruins in Central America and they will realize how important the skull is to the Maya and the Aztecs. The skulls do not represent sacrifice as so many choose to believe. Instead, they represent strength and knowledge.

The following information is not unlike the information that Hartley related. The Cherokee tell the story of 12 skulls with information from 12 planets. The Maya believe 13 skulls will return to their origin, the Mayan lands.

For Hunbatz, his experience with the skulls began early in life. The following is his story as he told me prior to studying in Mexico with him. Since English is his third language, I have taken the liberty of editing for easier understanding while maintaining the integrity and teachings of a Mayan elder.

As a representative of the Mayan Tradition, I consider it important to tell you what my Mayan Teacher and uncle, Don Beto, taught me about the crystal skulls. I remember some of his wise teachings, as for instance, one occasion when we were sitting watching the waters of the cenote in Wenk'al; my uncle suddenly stood up, and walked up to me finally stopping behind me. He asked me to stare at my face reflected on the water's surface for some time and he also told me that he would be watching me at the distance.

I obeyed his command and looked at my face's reflex on the water's surface for some time. Due to the solar light I noticed that sometimes my reflection changed its color from white to transparent occasionally. During this time, there was a moment when I started to have fun because of the different colors and forms my reflection adopted. It was so amusing to see how one of my ears stretched out, or how one of my eyes seemed to disappear, but with the course of time, I felt as if I were entering an unknown dimension and then I became a little scared.

But the scariest moment was when I saw another face's reflection next to mine on the water's surface. My first thought was that it was my uncle's face reflecting on the water, too. But when I turned around I could see my uncle Don Beto sitting down on my left side at about 15 meters away from me. He had been sitting on the same spot waiting for me. Even though I was so puzzled and scared, I looked back at the water's surface and then, I got really surprised! My face had turned into a skull. The most strange is that right in that moment I began to feel so calm and relaxed and after some minutes I saw how the skull became transparent and it could have been said that I began a trip through the skull's eyes and I saw many things. Perhaps it was my own skull that trans-

ported me into this wonderful trip, I am not quite sure about it, but what I can tell you for sure is that I saw many things in that trip. Someday I will write all these experiences I had in a book. I was still wandering in that dimension when I suddenly felt some pats on my back and I heard a voice telling me,

"Hunbatz!, Hunbatzl, Hunbatz!, Come back!, Come back!, Come back!"

Then I saw my uncle Don Beto looking and sweetly smiling at me and then he said: "Hunbatz, today you have been in the dimension the crystal skulls use to contact us. When you become older you will meet many people who will show you many of these skulls, but whenever you touch one, always remembers this magic moment you have just lived here in Wenk'a. He then he went on: "Today you traveled in the crystal skulls' dimension, if by any chance in the future you make ceremonies, think of this magic moment and the skulls will automatically reconnect with this sacred place of Wenk'a.

Teachings from MY Guides

I am sharing meditative information from 2001, not in an attempt to place myself in the same arena as Harley and Hunbatz but rather to show that the information is universal and available to all who choose to receive it. My guides, through my meditation said:

> *Each skull came to Earth with a piece of knowledge. In the beginning, each was a thought or seed of life for a small living entity. It held the programming, as it were, for that life form. As these life forms proved they could exist in love, more skulls were placed on Earth with more*

information. The entities had the knowledge to know how to match the skulls to produce more complicated seeds and therefore more complicated life forms. Again, once they proved themselves, more skulls were placed upon the Earth. This process continued.

Today, the skulls being found have only a small fragment of information available. When the reader (psychic) sees the color, they will know the level of knowledge and can gather all skulls of similar color.

These colors are harmonic and toned to match a beam of the MANU NYMBA. This is why the MANU NYMBA is the root of all life. The MANU NYMBA has all the colors of skulls and tones given so long ago. When you look at the Chakras and that part of the organism, look at the knowledge that an entity needs at each level.

Each, as you know, is at a different level of sophistication. Separately, they are pure light and can live in part. They need all others to complete the organism as it was designed.

You are asking about love and light that is NOT in all entities. This is true. This is free will and choice. All entities have all knowledge to live in the light. Some choose not to. When the skulls come together, the re-programming will begin again and light will shine. It is sacred and pure.

As I look back at this writing, I am fascinated at the similarity amongst the three.

- Harley speaks of 12 planets and the gift of all knowledge.
- Hunbatz speaks of 13, containing cosmic knowledge.
- Hunbatz remembers the calmness when he saw the skull. His writing also speaks of the travels.
- Harley alluded to this calmness and the traveling.
- My writing talks about the completeness of information through the skulls.
- My writing does not use the word "calmness"; instead it uses the words "love".

'STAR' Johnsen-Moser, a gifted psychic, who has worked with many Crystal Skulls, speaks a foreign language when she worked with the skull -- **MAX**. This language is TAK, a 36,000 year old Tibetan language. It is named after the constellation Orion. The cultures of India, Africa and Japan have kept TAK and other similar languages secret.

She speaks of the love and power that she feels when she is working through this language. Most of the information which she receives is not shared as it is too soon for most of humanity to accept.

At this time I had only been introduced to Crystal Skulls through channeling and the mythology related in books. I understand that experts believe there are 2 *authentic* skulls in existence -- the Mitchell-Hedges and the British Museum skulls. I later learned that 13 exist, all originally found in Central America. This number has also changed.

The Truths

When I was in Mexico studying the skulls and the Mayan culture, there were 20 skulls present; not all fitting the traditional description of a crystal skull. Some of these were large, human size and others were smaller models.

Since an authentic skull is purported to be life-size, molded out of a single piece of ancient clear quartz crystal with no evidence of tool markings, we can be confident that some of these 20 were created in a laboratory.

In July 2001 Barbara Marciniak, a channel of the Pleiades, answered a question from the audience at a public Vancouver forum about the number of skulls on Earth. The response was there were so many skulls on Earth that if they were gathered together, a human being could not handle the combined energy.

When I first heard this, I was not aware of the many pyramids around the world and the importance of the skulls being returned to each one. I also wonder if they were referring to skulls that are truly mystical or skulls carved out of a variety of stones with current tool technology.

Here are six of the most famous skulls in the world today. Perhaps they will help clarify the issues in each person's mind.

Mitchell-Hedges

Perhaps the most famous Skull is the **Mitchell-Hedges** Crystal Skull. While it's true origin has been kept secret, the most popular story is that it was *discovered* in British Honduras in the 1920s during an archaeological excavation.

One story was that as a surprise gift for the leader's daughter 17th birthday, it was placed in some ruins so she could discover it. At the time of writing this in 2002, the daughter, Anna Mitchell-Hedges, is still living in Canada. Until recently, she toured with her skull so that people could see and study it. She calls it the "Skull of Love" while the Maya call it "The Skull of Doom, or Death." If we look back into the Mayan culture, death is but a gateway to love and birth.

While I have not met Anna and only have what has been written as testimony, every time I receive information about this skull and his caretaker, I come away with a delightful feeling of gentle love.

He weighs 11.7 lbs. (5.3 kg) 5 in. high (12 cm), 5 in. wide and 7 in. (18 cm) long, making him quite a bit smaller than the Smithsonian skull of 31 lbs. MITCHELL-HEGES is one of the few skulls that have been examined by Hewlett Packard Laboratories (HP). These tests took place in the late 1970s in California. The results showed that the skull was made out of a single piece of quartz with no evidence of machine markings or modern hand tools. Another surprising result was that:

> "...the skull was not only made from a single piece of natural quartz, but from 'piezo-electric' silicon dioxide, precisely the type of naturally occurring quartz that is so widely used in modern electronics..."

The results further showed

> "...the properties of some kinds of quartz were only discovered towards the end of the nineteenth century... This means that this type of quartz means that it actually has a positive and negative polarity, just like a battery.

Earlier in this book, I referred to the polarity of the crystal cluster and the importance to balance. It was also important for accessing the MANU NYMBA information by the body. We now discover that the skulls have the same polarity.

Whenever I have held a crystal skull, I am always driven to place one hand on the forehead and the other at the back, near the base of the skull. As I read further about the HP tests, I discovered there was a reason for my actions and response. They found:

> "...like all piezo-electric quartz, the crystal skull is anisotropic in this as well as every other respect, which is to say that all of its properties, other than its mass, are different in every direction. In the case of its electrical properties, its precise orientation is defined by its X-Y axis, in other words, it can carry an electric current, but only in six particular directions relative to this X-Y axis. In any other direction, it acts as an insulator.
>
> In this case, the scientists found that it was 'vertically piezo- electrically oriented', which is to say that its X-Y axis runs directly through **the center of the skull, from top to bottom** (the bold text is my choice). This means that if you apply an electric charge to the top of the skull, not only does its shape change in the process, but also the electric current passes from the very top of the skull's head straight down to the Earth below. In the case of squeezing the skull to generate electricity, strangely enough, if you reverse

the direction of the pressure, the direction of electrical polarity in the crystal also reverses."

Usually, a caretaker spends a large amount of time getting to know his or her skull. I suspect that through this study, a caretaker learns how and when to apply pressure, depending upon the information. Could this be one reason why some are used as an information source and others used for healing?

British Museum Skull

The next on my list of *authentic* skulls is the **British Museum skull**. According to museum records, it was purchased from Tiffany's, New York, in 1898. Beyond this, the story of the origin remains another mystery. In the late 20th century, with permission of their owners, the British Museum conducted tests on several skulls. Their purpose was to find out their age, the source of the quartz and how were they made. As a result, they discovered the quartz was not old, probably coming from Brazil. The teeth showed wheel markings making the skull post-Columbian (15th century) and carved with European technology. Consequently, it was a 'modern fake'. It may be a fake in scientific and archeological terms, but it is still a remarkable feat. This skull is now displayed at London's Museum of Mankind.

Smithsonian Institute

In 1960, an Aztec skull, reported as once part of the Mexican President's collection, was purchased in Mexico City, Mexico. This skull was later donated anonymously to the **Smithsonian National Museum of American History.** One of the suspected reasons for its title, "The Cursed Skull," was a report about one of the owners committing suicide after experiencing several personal disasters.

Another possible reason is that it is ugly, almost ominous in appearance. It was hollow and yet weighed approximately 31 lbs (14 kg). Some consider it to be the largest known crystal skull, measuring 10" (25cm) high by 8.25" (21cm) wide.

This skull, like the British Museum skull, showed signed of wheel markings. Unlike the British Museum skull, they could not confirm the origin of the crystal.

Regardless of whether this was another "fake" or not, cursed or not, it still captivates the audiences who searched out the display in the Smithsonian Museum.

Max

MAX is known as a healing skull. Owned by Joanne and Carl Parks in Houston, Texas, he is larger than the Mitchell-Hedges skull and smaller than the Smithsonian, weighing in at 18 lbs (8 kg). He is best described as looking cloudy with half the face clear and many imperfections throughout the skull. Although there were these imperfections, the skull was carved out of one large piece.

The skull came into the Parks' lives through a Tibetan monk, Norbu Chen. They visited him when their young daughter was diagnosed with cancer. Through Chen and Max, her life was extended several years. When Norbu Chen died, he gave the skull to Joanne and Carl. Apart from saying it came from Guatemala, he would say nothing more; one day they would learn the secret. To my knowledge, only part of the secret has been revealed, thanks to Nick Nocerino, but joy comes to many who come into contact with MAX.

Today, Joanne and Carl travel with MAX holding workshops and meetings giving others an opportunity to meet MAX and feel the joy. Psychic people, such as 'STAR' Johnsen-Moser and Nick Nocerino have worked with the skull.

Star, a healer, workshop leader and medium, works with crystals to heal individuals and help people on their spiritual journey.

Nick, owner of **Sha Na Ra**, had a description of a skull given to him some time ago. For many years he searched for this elusive skull. Finally, in the early 1980s, he finally found MAX. Through Nick, Joanne discovered the strength of her skull and enjoys the joy to this day.

Joanne and Carl brought MAX to England for the British Museum tests. For some unknown reason, the representative from the British Museum would not comment about the skull.

Despite several attempts to get information, none was forthcoming. If there was any consolation, Max was not the only skull whose authenticity was not verified. The experts at the British Museum also would not comment on the authenticity of Nick Nocerino's skull -- Sha Na Ra.

Sha Na Ra

Nick Nocerino, considered today as one of the leading experts was introduced to crystal skulls and their energy when he was eight years old; not unlike Hunbatz Men. At that time, he looked into a mirror and saw a skull staring back at him. Normally this could be terrifying for a child of any age. However thanks to his Grandmother, he learned to understand and use the gift he had been given. For over half a century, Nick works with various skills using his psychic abilities, especially scrying -- a method of seeing visions within a clear crystal.

Today, his personal skull – Sha Na Ra, provides healing for others and information for all. He came upon this skull in 1959 while working on an undisclosed dig in Mexico. From the pictures, it appears slightly larger than Anna Mitchell-Hedge's skull, 13 lbs. (6kg). It is clear quartz with a soft yellow hue displaying prominent cheekbones.

While he believed **Sha Na Ra** was old, at least as old as the Aztecs, he was anxious to have the age confirmed through the British Museum testing. Unfortunately, like **MAX**, the scientific team who conducted the tested refused to comment on Sha Na Ra.

Parisian Skull

Our sixth and final skull was donated to the Trocadero Museum in Paris and was already part of the collection when their written records began in the late 1800s.

In the 1990s, Chris Morton and Ceri Thomas participated in the planning and skull selection for the British Museum testing. They asked the Parisian Museum if they could include the skull from that museum.

The Parisian museum declined, stating that they had already conducted numerous scientific tests themselves. They were convinced that it was 14th or 15th century, stylized after the ancient Aztecs and their neighbor the Mixtecs.

The testing went forward without this skull.

Not wishing to contradict the experts, there is some conjecture that this skull may have been carved in Germany; Idar-Oberstein, is a small town. This town was a well-known carving center with many apprentice schools. Apparently, it was a challenge for students to carve skulls. We do know that around the time in question, other skulls *were* carved there.

Even today skulls are coming out of this small town as was confirmed by a present-day carver. Hans-Jürgen Henn. When asked about the skulls he has carved, he commented:

> *"The stones tell us how they want to be carved and cut, and this can make things a little difficult. You see this stone, I guess, was sleeping for a while before he told us what he wanted to be."*

If a present-day carver senses this, then surely other carvers over the years have had the similar conversations with other stones. Personally, I do not think it is that important to know for sure whether the Parisian Skull is from the 15th century or from Germany in the 20th century.

The stone itself is old. The carver / craftsman had the skills to interpret the message; the important part. We need to be ready to accept it in whatever form.

- What information is mankind ready to receive?
- Are they really the Mayan skulls returning to the Maya land?
- Do they really assist in the healing of individuals and if so, how?
- Is there prophetic information that is coming through?

The answer to all of these questions depends on the perspective of the person asking.

Now is a time when we must acknowledge that the available information is beyond what archaeological and scientific research can give us.

The general agreement is that the skulls first appear on the Earth Plane in Central America region. Since other Crystal Skulls are being kept secret we can't prove otherwise. There is a connection between languages that prove a link between the peoples. Here are a couple of examples.

One: The English word *Skull*, according to the Webster's New Collegiate Dictionary, Skull is Middle English, derived from Scandinavia origins. In Mayan, Skull is **skool,** with **SK** meaning travel and **KU** meaning body. Together, it is "Traveling Body". It is interesting just how similar the two words Skull and Skool are, but not surprising when we remember that the Crystal Skulls traveled to Africa. From there they and their related teachings went from Africa, through Europe or Asian into the Scandinavia region.

Two: The letter "T" is important to the Maya, as seen on many of their temple walls. Valmiki, writer of the Hindu books *Ramayana* and *Mahabharata,* states that around 2700 BCE, the Naga Maya brought their culture to India, introducing the knowledge of "T".

Again, if the cultural, knowledge went to India, so would the key representative tool, the Crystal Skull.

There are other, more detailed examples but two illustrate the potential scope of the travels. These are the truth.

Summary

Skull strength and power contributed to environmental events while I was in Mexico. While I was there during the hurricanes in September, 2002, we had planned a full moon ceremony for the equinox. Since we were in the middle of a powerful storm (the edge of the hurricane) we decided to hold the ceremony indoors.

However, five minutes before the appointed time, the rain stopped. The clouds opened. It stayed that way for approximately 15 minutes. The clouds closed and the rain started again as if someone slammed a door and turned on a tap. The region experienced severe devastation, not simply from one storm proceeding as customary, nor from several storms one right after another but from a single storm hovering overhead for 12 hours. Apparently, this is very unusual for a region that experiences hurricanes annually.

We were in Mexico studying the messages of the Crystal Skulls, asking for the return to Mexico according to their prophecy. The presence of 20 skulls in one place opened the clouds showing us the full moon. These 20 skulls caused the storm to hover in one location. A single skull is powerful but 20 together regardless of size or shape is even more powerful.

This to my knowledge, was the first time that a large number of skulls were gathered together; the beginning of the communication <u>between</u> the skulls and <u>with</u> the skulls. According to the Maya, the skulls will come together to give the knowledge and strength. We saw the strength that week. The knowledge is coming.

When there is killing, or death during the time of the merging of the Crystal Skulls, it throws the balance off. Understanding that the MANU NYMBA is within the Crystal Skulls, the people present and the trees surrounding the ceremonies, you can understand that the balance is extremely delicate.

To allow the flow of knowledge, crystal clusters connected to the MANU NYMBA cannot be compressed. If this happens, the release of the piezo-electric energy is reduced.

I see this energy flow every day as I have a small skull on my desk. When I hold it, the information comes through is much stronger.

Should the reader want to participate, or prove, skull energy, I suggest that they get hold of a skull. On the next equinox, sit in a quiet space with the skull in the lap. Place the left hand on the base of the back of the skull and the right hand on the forehead, over the 3rd eye. Go into a meditative stage and discover what information awaits you. Perhaps, you will discover a piece of the information that is waiting the human race.

EARTH DESIGNS

> *"When you make the finding yourself, even if you're the last person on Earth to see the light, you'll never forget it"*—Carl Sagan

Whenever we utter the words "crop circles," our thoughts immediately travel to England and the elaborate creations or mysterious hoaxes found there, However, if I used the words "earth designs," most people conjure up a mystical image, more exotic than even the most intricate crop circles.

Unfortunately, the media of the 20th century concentrated upon the crop circle phenomenon, blinding us to other, older and just as mystical earth designs. If I asked the question: -- Are crop circles and the Nasca lines similar? The answer is usually "NO".

These same people however, would agree that there was possible a link between other unexplained edifices on the Earth. A label limits our visualization. Therefore, I will use the term "Earth Designs" for this section and will use crop circle only when I am referring to the specific phenomenon.

Previously in other sections I referred to the information or messages that appear on our Earth. The signs needed interpretation, perhaps by an anthropologist or a linguist. The Trees and Crystal skulls needed somebody cognizant of the energy vibrating from the source.

The Earth Designs require both of these, an interpreter and an energy reader, sometimes the same person, sometimes not. Since everything on our planet and beyond originates from its own personalized MANU NYMBA, which also carries the CLP (Cosmic Life Pattern). understanding the MANU NYMBA or accepting the principle the crystalline energy becomes the nucleus of communication.

But how can we possibly understand or interpret the messages; we are not multilingual? The answer is relatively simple.

We understand them today because our consciousness is rising. We are learning many languages without being aware. What is not clear however is which is which -- the root or the result.

Are we absorbing these languages because our consciousness is rising, leading to a better balanced MANU NYMBA or the opposite? Personally, I am not concerned about the cause or effect. I like the result and want to keep it, and I am sure many others will agree with me.

These internal adjustments allow us to see an increasing number of Earth Designs. There are more earth designs appearing, plus we are seeing each one in more detail. The communication possibilities soar.

Earth designs are means of communication from people, entities or even energies originating from beyond, or from within our planet. Frequently, they are from beings not as evolved, unfortunately also sometimes not as benevolent either. Fortunately, it is the etheric ones who transmit messages through our thoughts and subconscious.

Occasionally however, these latter energies do resort to placing images such as earth designs on the Earth; a minor complication. This is simply a desperate attempt to get our attention and find a language that everyone can understand.

For the lay person, discerning whether a message is from an evolved energy or not can be difficult and this is where the energy reader excels. Through this emitted energy, this person will know how we should respond.

It is important, though that we do not ignore our current designs simply because we are not sure of the source. They are still of interest as they show how the communication has changed over the eons, much like being open to archaeological research.

By turning to the ancient peoples and their elders or wise ones, we receive some answers. The ancient peoples of our world passed stories and myths from one generation to the next. They recognized the importance of remembering them so that others could learn from them. We have only to look at their stories to realize that earth designs told them a great deal.

The Hopi of the United States, the Maya of Mexico and the Waitaha of New Zealand are only a few of the indigenous peoples who have told stories rising out of earth designs.

Dwellers today are more aware of the dietary patterns and lifestyles the indigenes today.

Many readers will immediately respond with thoughts like: "What about distant cultures? They haven't changed their eating habits." This is true, they have not. However, change can also be defined as "rigorously adhering to a historical lifestyle."

Both Western society and distant cultures made unconscious decisions that led to a better balanced MANU NYMBA, the right one for the individual.

The resulting end product is a host body with much more clarity; clarity in vision and clarity in hearing. This lucidity allows us to absorb purer colors and harmonic tones.

I compare it to a deaf person suddenly being able to hear again. It is important to remember that evolution has many paths. All this opens the door to experiencing earth designs previously invisible to us. Instead of simple clarification and answers, we frequently get a bigger conundrum, an exciting event for the viewer.

Generally, people associate earth designs as coming from spaceship passengers visiting in the night; some do. Earth designs involving heavy objects probably came from the humans living at the time of their creation or from other worlds. However, what I propose at this time is that we change our thinking slightly and consider *all* crop circles as originating from the crystalline energy beneath the surface.

Crystalline energy vibrates in accordance with the entire universe, forming a communication system predating humans. Humans did not invent it.

When a crop circle is created, the crystal energy vibrates in a pattern that, they hope, will be understood. This harmonic humming is what is heard in some of the crop circles. We are now witnessing just one side of a communication network probably created for our benefit.

Some Earth Designs carry information from our historical past. Designs such as Stonehenge may be credited to beliefs from long ago but where did the concepts originate? They carried their own form of DNA or MANU NYMBA. The answer was within the formation.

Other Earth Designs such as the lava caves of the world carry information from *beyond* our present world. All these are profound. Let us not forget though, **what is within is beyond** and vice versa.

Everything is one.

Viewing one side of this puzzle, we learn our history and evolutionary path. Viewing another side introduces us to communication throughout the entire cosmos. We now need to ask ourselves; what can we learn from these images? What is it they are trying to teach us? Individually, we receive one answer. Linking more than one design together shows us a different answer. Then there are earth designs that need to be studied from both perspectives, individually and networked. The network can be an alignment of two or it might be several. In the network, each design provides a small piece of a large puzzle.

One example of this is a recent gathering of the crystal skulls in Mexico. Here, the crystal skulls were nothing more than a portable earth design, a portable crystalline energy. At this time, the purpose was to awaken the Mayan wisdom. A single skull held close to a specific charka offered healing power. However, placing several in a triangle or circle formation around a person or a temple increased the power substantially. Placing them near cenotes -- sacred wells -- magnified the energy even more. While the energy of a single skull lingered, we found that the powerful energy of many skulls could be felt for some time. Participants carried this energy home even without the physical presence of the skulls.

On this particular tour we were privileged to enjoy the presence of many skulls but we must remember that it does not require multiple skulls to alter the energy.

A single skull used in conjunction with any other earth design produces the same effect. The person or people present will benefit similar results. Today, caretakers of the skulls can continue with the work by placing them near or in other earth designs.

Aligning multiple earth designs is not limited to the wealthy traveler or gifted healers. Each one of us can align two Earth Designs whenever we choose. When it is done with love and intent, it will almost always be successful. If you don't have access to two earth designs in close proximity, you simply visit one and create the second, completing the partnership.

For example, if you are near one crop circle, then drawing a pattern in the sand or bringing a drawing from home of another is appropriate. What you create or bring will depend upon the earth design and your intent. Here it helps having an understanding of the message cast by the earth design. If you are near a monolith, then you might want to bring a stone object with you. Of course this does not give permission to damage the stone monolith.

Standing or sitting in line with each object brings two different gifts. One allows us to go within and discover what is stored within our being, the MANU NYMBA being an example. The other gives access to the universal knowledge, especially from the Pleiades, knowledge we share with others.

Both the MANU NYMBA and Pleiadian wisdom are founded upon love and kindness. The energy and information will flow regardless of the objects we see or use. All earth designs increase the power/energy to access everything we have, love, compassion, and healing ability. All the energy is within us, keeping our bodies healthy.

It is also beyond us, because we are able to access other sources and give healing energy to others who have not yet learned to heal themselves and/or trust themselves. A gentle reminder – all knowledge, even if it comes from the universe is available through the planet's structure.

This knowledge is love. Once we accept that all knowledge *is* love, we realize that any knowledge we perceive as technical must have had a different beginning. History may have taught us that the Atlantis culture was technical and the cultures from Lemuria were centered on healing and loving.

However, what I see when I hear this statement is that people are only looking at the end result. At some time, though all cultures from the Lemuria and Atlantis worlds were identical, filled with love and compassion. Unfortunately, as power and greed spread throughout a region, the intent changed. Self-indulgence flooded over the original intent with all the love and compassion.

What does this have to do with earth designs? When we look at ancient designs, their origin was based in love even though intervening cultures used them for other purposes. Everything I have read or been told says that original peoples on this planet originated from the Pleiades, including Atlantis and Lemuria.

While it is impossible to explore all of the mysterious earth designs on Earth at this time, we can look at select designs that have been studied by others. Using the MANU NYMBA information, perhaps the reader will receive new insight.

Meridians Ley lines or Great circles of the Earth

The lines connecting the earth designs of this world are strong and potent. These three names, meridians, ley lines, and great circles all reflect this description.

Ley lines are defined as *a path of power extending around the world.*

Similarly, meridians are electrical nerve fluid lines (*power, or chi*) that behave according to the universal movement of the planets, making them a conjunctive part of the universe.

The great circles simply cut the earth in half, crisscrossing countless times to form a web just as strong and powerful as that of the spider.

When we overlay the meridians and ley lines onto these great circles, we observe power lines of tremendous force.

The next step is adding all the acupuncture points of Chinese medicine to our map. Chinese medicine teaches that the acupuncture points on the ear access the entire body. Furthermore, researchers identified England as the ear of the Earth's body. This implies there is a vast conduit (meridian) system just under the Earth's surface.

Now we know why there have been so many unexplained designs in this region. This also supports the suggestion that the earth designs are from within the earth. The meridians of the body have energy or power flowing through them, needing a reliable exit point; as does the Earth. However, if we continue assuming the earth designs are from beyond the Earth, then these acupuncture points are simply gateways or portals for the energy to *enter* the planet. Either way, this is a pathway for spreading information around the globe. It also explains why ancient cultures built temples along the lines. Still, I do find it strange that humans can comprehend a link between objects of a similar period or culture but cannot appreciate the possibility of a linkage stretching farther back in time.

Are the pyramids of Egypt connected to the temples of Mexico or Easter Island?

Is there a connection between the Ica stones of Peru and the Rongo- rongo tablets of Easter Island?

Earth designs can be viewed in various ways. In current times, we see designs such as crop circles. They hint of a communication source much more sophisticated than we are today. We need to look at the possibility that all earth designs came *out* of the Earth's crust, not thrust upon it by an unknown force from beyond.

This explains the linkage between designs, since energy flowing beneath the surface carries forth the information available through each design.

It explains the commonalities of ancient stories from peoples who lived long ago.

It explains the evidence of a sophisticated communication source. I suspect the purpose of all communication and information is guidance and assistance. The stories and myths evolving from the designs and the residents of long ago support this idea.

This also explains the more complicated designs we see today. As our awareness rises, so does the sophistication of patterns. As more patterns are explored, the more aware we become of the similarities and links amongst all the earth designs.

Unfortunately, space does not permit us to study all earth designs so we will be presenting only a few. Hopefully you will discover how connections evolved and explore independently.

Crop Circles Designs

So far in this section we have talked about the broad topic of earth designs of the world. Lately though, Crop Circles have been a title of choice. Although there have been a few hoaxes uncovered, they are few in quantity and not relevant. Instead, we are looking at genuine crop circles that could not be explained by scientists. Who placed them on Earth and what do they mean?

The chosen drawings came from one of three sources.

Firstly, a comprehensive book written by Judith Moore and Barbara Lamb, -- "*Crop Circles Revealed*".

The second source is a book by Freddy Silva, -- "*SECRETS in the FIELDS, the Science and Mysticism of Crop Circles*".

My last source is a computer website titled www.earthfiles.com.

The design selections were completely intuitive. I was surprised to discover that except for the website selections, they were all from one county in England, Wiltshire county. The ones selected from the Website originated in Ohio, USA. Out of these latter ones, three were similar to each other *and* a circle found in the Wiltshire County, England in 1994.

While more than ninety percent of the world's crop circles have appeared in what was old Wessex. Wiltshire County only has about forty percent. Perhaps this concentration can be attributed to the prevalence of Celtic folklore.

Laiolin, a spirit entity from the Council of Aborha, tells us that England is chosen for so many crop circles because "*whoever controls Point Zero has tremendous power over the planet.*" (Crop Circles Revealed, P119) Time will tell.

Crop Circles were verbally reported throughout time. However, few were recorded until the last thirty-five years of the 20th century. The interest exploded in the 1990s after scientists caught sight of photographs in local newspapers. The ones chosen for this publication originated during the 10 year span before the millennium.

Since this selection was intuitive, I studied each one and recorded my emotions and any insightful thoughts. It was only then that I looked at the comments in the two books which I used as reference.

The first one came from *The Cereologist* --Summer 1991, and is titled **Barbury Castle** –

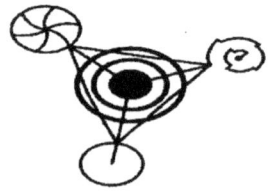

This Crop Circle was discovered July 17, 1991 near Swindon, Wiltshire, England. As I looked at the drawing, I am drawn to the three dimensional tetrahedron in the center and the power it holds. I also see a combination of the signs that I have been shown.

The circle at the upper left contains three curves similar to the sun cycle illustrated earlier in the sign section. Not only are they telling me that the viewer is on the right path but they are completely balanced – three curves in perfect symmetry. I also noted the progression into balance. We move from a single, solitary circle (lower), to one with equal harmonic divisions to the third one that is opening the self to the universe.

In the center is a multiple ring. After reading about the Cydonia area on Mars and Erol Torun's studies of the tetrahedron, ring and geographical areas, I was intrigued about the energy phenomenon. If the placement of this geometric form coordinating with the poles can create an energy eruption (a volcano), what message was this formation giving us? It is also noteworthy that the Cydonia area of Mars was discovered in 1976, 15 years before this particular design appeared. It is possible that it appeared in other regions as someone tried to get our attention. When we are in perfect symmetry and open ourselves to the universe, we are then given all the power and energy required (the shapes inside the three outer drawings).

When I went into the book *Crop Circles Revealed*, I got two interpretations, one by the entity Laiolin and the other by Judith Moore, the body host of Laiolin.

Laiolin says:

> *"This crop circle is the balancing resonator for the cosmic law of perfection through imperfection. This is the law of radical discover, the divine principle of balance of unequal counterpoints with the matrix of divine creation and evolution."*

Judith Moore comments:

> *"This is a three-dimensional design depicted in two dimensions on flat ground. The tetrahedron incorporates a circle and rings and branches out to three differing wheel-like shapes, each with its own symbolic meanings. The whole pattern is similar to sixteenth-century symbols for alchemical formulas and sacred geometry. It is one version of Mandelbrot fractals."*

Judith Moore brings a complex identity to the Earth designs. Her higher self is Laiolin and is also a conscious channel of Laiolin. Laiolin is a 13th dimensional ambassador of the Great Central Sun with an ET existence on the Arcturian Mother Ship.

Laiolin is also a member of the Council of Aborha, Keeper of the Records of RA and has the responsibility to bring high level communications through to assist the third dimensional earth persons with their evolutionary development.

Freddy Silva delves deeply into sacred geometry in his book. He spent some time studying the magnetism and spinning of circles. In particular, he pondered over the ratchet shape of the smaller right circle. Each side of the open circle can be viewed as a step. Each *step* of the ratchet circle deviates from magnetic north by 4 degrees (Silva, P131).

This generates a swirling or spinning motion. Further on in his book, page 153, he quotes scholar John Mitchell.

Mitchell wrote:

> *It demonstrates the principle of Three in One by means of a central circle which exactly contains the combined areas of the three circles*

around it. Moreover, the sum of all the four circular areas in the crop glyph is 31680 square feet....In traditional cosmology, 31680 was taken to be the measure around the sub-lunary world, and the early Christian scholars calculated the number 3168 as emblematic of Lord Jesus Christ. The same number was previously applied to the name of a leading principle in the pagan religion.

Dr. Benoit Mandelbrot is a professor of Mathematics at Yale University.(www.math.yale.edu)

Hakpen Hill --Summer 1999

There are many hills that have become owners of earth designs. This particular one was discovered July 4, 1999 near Broad Hinton, just below Hakpen Hill, also in Wiltshire County.

Freddy Silva notes that this hill is one of locations that is rich in chalk, a form of limestone which is the same mineral as the famous chalk horse. Before reading more of his comments I couldn't help but wonder if this is one of the explanations for numerous crop circles.

Then I read further in his book. Silva, along with numerous other investigators, discovered that 87% of the crop circles over a ten year period were on chalk land (Silva, P120).

Chalk soil is present when there is water close to the surface. The two combined indicates a low magnetic field. The scientific mind can explore more of these studies in his book. For the lay person, it is sufficient to acknowledge this as a feature of the English designs. We can only speculate on designs found elsewhere.

He mentions nine spirals while I only see 6. However, in the photograph, you can see three faint lines that follow the curve tip to the broad part of the next swirl. Possibly this constitutes the nine. But, since they are faint and don't match the pattern of the other lines, I am not including them at this time.

As I viewed this circle I was aware of three factors.

Firstly, the swirling image reminded me of the central energy we saw in the Barbury Castle's design.

Secondly, I was pulled to the closing of the ends of each of the three paired swirls.

Finally, the pairs come together in the center (note dots) and then the lines part again, suggesting perhaps that some of them have a circular pathway and the others have an oval one.

I also got a strong feeling of swirling out of control. Moving my eye out from the center to the ends brings up several images.

The first is the sharp points swirling in a stabbing motion.

The next image was the numbers 6 and 3 swirling in, out and around. Because I have received numerous pieces of information connecting the Maya culture to other planetary cultures, I looked into their world for a possible explanation. Just what is the significance of the number of swirls and lines in the Mayan world?

In the Mayan culture, the number 3 means – intensity, opening of the spirit world.

The number 6 means passing of old, outmoded things.

When the three pathways are closed at the end, I sense they are telling us that we are NOT opening the door to the spirit world, plus the energy is intense. Since the six lines are paired up, and closed, we are also not getting rid of the old and outmoded things.

As I look at the center, I felt I was in the middle of a natural disaster such as a tornado or volcano. Since this wasn't tornado season, I decided to look at volcanoes of our world, another powerful natural event.

The website, www.volcanoworld.org studied the volcanic action in 1999 and matched it to the great circles of the Earth. There were only 4 eruptions after July 4th on the planet; two of which were on the same great circle line from England.

The first of these was in Telica Nicaragua, August 11th. The second was Ruapehu Peak on the North Island of New Zealand, erupting on September 13th, 1999.

The crop circle was formed on July 4th, 1999, last quarter of the moon phase. Both Telica and Ruapehu erupted on a new moon.

In my first book, *Inner Bridges*, the channeled information spoke of the atmospheric energy being heavier at full moon and lighter at new moon. Does this lightness apply to earth designs and volcanoes?

I couldn't help but feel sad realizing we have all the information available to us but we are not listening to the spirit messengers and end up swirling in uncontrolled confusion. Unfortunately, I also cannot help but wonder whether we are occasionally the cause of the volcanic eruptions on the Earth. Is this what the Hakpen Hill design is telling us?

My first review of this crop circle seemed a little dark. Consequently, I decided to look at the swirling energy from a different angle, a more positive one. Instead of seeing it as a potential disaster, we can also see birth. When a twirl slows down, we are seeing the same effect as the MER-KA-BA slowing down and giving birth to the MANU NYMBA, the internal entity.

A volcano is also a beginning of life, simply in a different form.

The particular great circle that connects these three events crosses the land of MU, otherwise known as Lemuria. Was this Earth design telling us that information was being given to us from the land Lemuria through these two volcanoes?

There were actual earth designs originally in the white horse. These have been wiped away by people over the decades in their attempts to keep the horse pristine.

On one of the great circles we find four countries positioned Brazil, New Zealand and Western Australia and Tibet. There is no evidence at this time, but there is a link between the Waitaha of New Zealand, the Real People of Australia and the ancient Tibet.

All of these are ancient wisdoms and we will also find strong crystals and volcanoes. In addition, the crystal skulls are found in all of these locations. What I discern is the crop circle in England was telling us of the swirling energy of the volcanoes and the gifts of crystals that await discovery.

Look-Alikes across the Ocean

May 28, 1994
Avebury, England 2º W 50.5North

August 15, 2000
Whitefish, Montana
114º W 48ºN

October 2, 2003
Bainbridge, Ohio
41.2ºN 81º W

When I went to this particular website -- www.earthfiles.com, I read about concerns about these possibly being hoaxes. However, I did my own *intuitive* checking and the designs are legitimate. Although there were several other designs sighted near the Ohio mounds, I selected these designs since several factors caught my attention.

Point One:

As pioneers headed west, ancient burial Indian mounds were routinely found. Until the 1980s there was no projected age of these mounds. However, since the recorded nations in this region were the Adena Indians dating back to 1,000BC and the Hopewell Indians dated from 100BC to 500 AD, it was assumed that the mounds were a similar age.

I suspect, however, there were many, much older cultures in this region. I base part of this supposition on the recorded age of inhabitants in other areas. They are proven to be prehistoric; therefore cannot these mounds and people be equally ancient? There is no evidence suggesting a reason for these to be a different period.

I mention these mounds at this time because of the close proximity to the Ohio and Montana designs. One of the designs shown above was found just four miles east of Seip Mound. Another was a little closer to Seip Mound, only two miles away. The third one was a half mile from Serpent Mound.

The usual approach to the study of earth designs is observing whether the designs were made *near* a sacred mound.

Instead of a traditional sacred mound, if we look at the great earth circles or energy in the region, then the mounds were made according to the power of the region. It is the region, not the mound that is important; the designs are simply a more recent reflection.

We will probably never know how many designs were created near original mound sites but looking at the great circle system tells us that similar energy centers exist along each pathway.

One of the great circles takes us from England, through Greenland, into Ohio and Montana and over to Australia. We already see that this design was important enough to duplicate it numerous times through crop circles. Therefore, I hypothesize that there are other similar designs along circle routes conveying important information. We just need an interpreter.

Point Two:

The designs grew in complexity over the years. In England, we started with empty outer circles and six swirling lines inside the big one. Next we see the Montana design with small solid circles inside the outer ones. The curved lines flow evenly and neatly into the center. The Ohio design includes small geometric shapes in each of the outer circles and adds an additional three circles.

One of the archeological discoveries in the Ohio region was the extensive use of geometric patterns on mound artifacts. This particular crop circle design integrated these shapes. We also know it is not just these three designs that grew in complexity but *all earth designs* of the planet.

Therefore, doesn't it make sense that the designs would follow the intelligent level of the region, using the knowledge of the inhabitants? Since the use of geometric patterns dates much farther back than 1000 years, I cannot help but question the age of the designs.

Point Three:

The third observation is the direction of the arms. Designs 3-b and 3- c swirl in a counter-clockwise motion while 3-a is directed clockwise. The ancient Greek symbol of sun in motion, **Triskelion** has three legs pointed in *counter-clockwise* directions. We know that *Ohio and Montana record more sunshine hours than Wiltshire, England.* Is there a link between sunshine hours and design formations?

The Celts and many other cultures adapted this symbol and called it **Celtic Triskele**. Today, we see this pattern on many works of art including robes, and coins. This particular pattern is a circle with three inner curved lines, linking the rim to the center. These lines are arched in a *clockwise* curvature, similar to the Wiltshire design.

Point Four:

Every time I sat down to write about these designs, I see, or hear, the word "SWASTIKA". I find this strange because the swastika has four arms and this particular earth designs only shows 3 arms. I began to understand that there are other designs, as yet undiscovered, that are connected to these three that *do* have the fourth arm. Nevertheless, I find the meaning of the swastika transferable: -- "good luck" or "to be good". In some literature the sign also means power or migration. Could it be that the signs be connected with shifts of power or change for humanity? It is important to note that the meaning used here is the original meaning, not that of the German Nazis.

Point Five:

As your understanding of the planet's network and connecting energies expands, so does the examination about the distance between these designs and projected extensions.

Is there a stronger, hidden connection we don't know about? The distance between the three designs is

   --England to Montana   ≈ 4,500 miles
   --Montana to Ohio   ≈ 2,000 miles
   -- Ohio to England   ≈ 3,600 miles

WITHIN & BEYOND: REVISITED

These distances are taken as the crow flies and are an approximation. When the three routes are drawn on a map, they form a scalene (unequally sided) triangle, one of the most common forms of triangles. The heart, or centroid point, of this triangle is in Newfoundland, Labrador, Quebec area of Canada. It is also close in shape to our star tetrahedron, home of the MANU NYMBA.

This region was the home of many ancient indigenous peoples such as Algonquin and Huron. In some way, I feel their wisdom is linked just as is all ancient cultures.

Again, it is important that the reader consider all types of Earth Designs, not just crop circle images.

There are some wonderful cave formations in this area. Newfoundland gives us the Corner Brook Caves, and Strawberry Hill. The Warsaw Caves are near Peterborough Ontario. Within every cave, not just these, we find tantalizing images along the walls and in the rocks at our feet.

Point Six:

As we extend the three lines connecting the three designs, we discover that the three lines are each part of a great circle. One leads to Ayers Rock in Australia with the other end in Russia. One circle also includes Dogon region in Africa. The third circle connects England, Montana and the Yonaguni ruins in the waters off the Western tip of Japan.

In the waters of Yonaguni off the most Western tip of Japan are underwater ruins of buildings and numerous formations. Divers have reported huge boulders, called Sun Rocks, resting on platforms. These platforms appear to have had human assistance plus there are cuneiform markings etched in the stone. Some of the researchers estimate these ruins to be approximately 12,000 years old.

Another link in this chain of power is Pohnpei Island in Micronesia. For the average tourist, the volcanic remains are nothing more than a hiking spot. However, Sokehs Rock is not an ordinary remnant of a volcano generates power and energy, much like the crop circles of England. Even looking at the picture, I am pulled to running my fingers over the side.

Also on the island, rather off shore underwater, are the Nan Madol ruins. More than 2,000 years old, the one exciting aspect of these ruins is the building structure. The walls look like log cabin walls. However, they are entirely of stone.

Point Seven:

Again the number 3 is evident. For indigenous people, it represents earth, sea and sky. The Celtic interpretation is life, death, and rebirth. In Western and Mayan cultures, the number 3 means – intensity, opening of the spirit world.

- **Alton Priors** -- June 19, 2000

This pattern appears sophisticated and playful. At first glance it might remind the viewer of a merry-go-round at a fair. However, as I looked more deeply, I realized that it is giving us a powerful, serious message through a playful arena.

One of reasons that circular designs are so prevalent and powerful is that the circle contains everything in our universe. There is no beginning and no end. It disseminates all knowledge equally.

As I looked at this design, I realized that it was carrying 8 facets of knowledge. The reader may challenge this, seeing sixteen instead. However, each piece of wisdom appears in both hemispheres. These knowledge facets are:

Crystal energy	Herbal healing
Cultures of the world	Spiritual messages
Ancient sites	Directions upon the planet
The arts	Geometric wisdom

As this wheel turns, it makes every facet available to the entire planet. Consequently, we must remember that when something, such as spiritual messages, is being disseminated on one side, it is also being collected on the opposite side. I tend to think of it as a polarity function.

The center of the wheel then has two roles -- dissemination of knowledge, wisdom and collection.

As this information came to me, I instantly went to a stagnant planet and a slow-moving MANU NYMBA. Immediately though, I saw the wheel rotating slowly, ensuring that no region is stuck with just one function. In addition, this turning is independent of the moon or the gravitation of the earth. It seems to rotate, or spin according to the evolution or dimensions of the population, providing equality or variety as needed. It is carrying and disseminating the entire CLP to all inhabitants.

Our world has been polluted and decimated in the twentieth century. Fortunately, we are changing, and research tells us the crystal content is increasing.

Another characteristic of this wheel is the fact that the focal point can be wherever we choose (or it chooses). There are vortexes all over the world. These are power or energy centers, drawing the power from surrounding regions. Living entities are also power centers. Ritualistic centers and ancient ruins are power centers. Again, all of these power or energy centers are both *di*verging and *con*verging points, depending upon the needs of the time.

I have heard about people gathering around a particular vortex, trying to reverse the flow. This is contrary to the overall plan of planet power.

If a vortex flow changes direction, it is for a specific reason and we should not intervene. I believe that this earth design was giving us important message. Whatever spiritual information we gather, it spreads from our thought waves in a wheel-like flow. Being a human being limits our abilities but they are in reality boundless. As such we are teachers. The lessons vary according to our plans but the answers are spread throughout the planet and subsequently, the universe.

An alternative way of looking at this wheel is discovering a new way of seeing the great circles of the globe. When we place the hub on a specific design, we then see connections between designs and the pathways.

For example, if we place the hub in the Hopi world, we connect Mesoamerica and Eastern Siberia and China. There are powerful resources in this area, all in the turning wheel.

Dr. Nan Lu in Lamb's book, states that this design is for correcting blood disorders and digestive problems. My answer to this is the longitudes are the life blood of the Earth and therefore must be clear energy running through them. When we look at the problems of the Earth from this approach, we can see how the trouble areas are linked. Conversely, the healthy, spiritual regions are also linked. Through this pattern, we can share the healing properties and cleanse the planet. As I read his observation, I realize how we tend to ignore the circulation and digestion functions of the body. We also ignore the communication around the planet at this subtle level.

Celtic cross designs

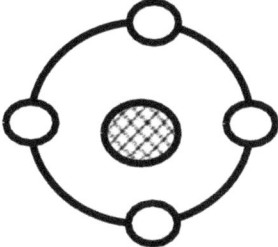

How often do we hear people dismissing a simple design in favor of the more elaborate creations? This is unfortunate because an uncomplicated design holds a great deal of information for us. Interestingly, in spite of the absence of enthusiasm there have been many similar patterns discovered around the world.

The official name of this sculpture is ***Celtic cross***, a formation used by many ancient peoples of the world, not just the Celts. We cannot include every design but there are several pertinent ones that I draw to your attention.

1. On July 25, 1990 in Morgan Hill, Wiltshire, England the first of two Celtic cross designs appeared. At this

time the new moon was on the 22nd. The second design appeared three weeks later that slightly overlap the first one. This one appeared one week *before the next new moon.*
2. On June 19th, 2000, 3 days *after the new moon,* the one shown above appeared in Milton Lilbourne.
3. On July 14th, 2001, seven days *before the new moon,* farmers in Russia discovered a similar design.
4. On August 6, 2002 another one in Howick, Quebec, Canada was formed, only two days *before the new moon.*

As I viewed these formations, I was immediately reminded of the four transition times of our year, summer and winter solstice and spring and fall equinox. Almost every primordial culture aligned their buildings or monuments to mark these calendrical events.

The ones that immediately come to mind are Stonehenge, Maya, Hopi, and Inca. The Milton Lilbourne design taken July 2000.

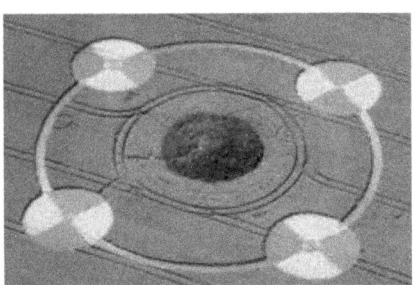

It was created 3 days after the new moon and one day *before* the summer solstice. Perhaps an astrologer student would find comparable synchronistic facts for the other designs.

The Milton Lilbourne design center is a fifteen foot Neolithic mound. Historically, archaeologists discovered that burial mounds and sacred sites were generally located at high electromagnetic energy centers. Therefore, I suspect that the other locations produce comparable high energy output.

When I look at these Celtic cross designs, I immediately envisage funnels coming from the earth, through each circle up to the sky, a conduit of energy flowing bi-directional from the core of the Earth to the universe. Again, this makes sense as I believe that all designs are created through the help of the Pleiadian people.

Another reason why this knowledge could resurface with this simple design is the six outer circles and the center one. The Pleiades are known as the "Seven Sisters"; one star is almost invisible.

This design is also the formation of the medicine wheel of the Native Americans. I am sure when the design appeared in Quebec, they did not think of it as a Celtic cross but rather a native message of great importance.

Usually, the messages are interpreted according to the indigenous people of the region. The creators of the designs know this and this could be the reason why certain designs are so popular around the globe.

One more aspect coming to me as I looked at this design was the visual connection forming a pyramid. This puzzled me but I have learned to accept that images come to my mind for specific reasons.

When you connect all four satellite circles with straight lines, visualize the center being higher and this mound forms a point, you have created a pyramid. I pondered the design and pyramid together, looking for a connection. Pyramids are used for worship and burial.

The Milton Lilbourne design center is a fifteen foot Neolithic mound created around an ancient burial mound. Many designs have been incorporated into Celtic ceremonies.

Pyramids are storage sites for important data. What are earth designs but communication devices for important data? This design then must be linked in some manner to the pyramids of the Earth.

The mystery continues: --

For almost three months in 2003 on a fairly regular frequency, I envisaged a similar design over the rain forest in Brazil. As you can imagine, in a dense forest such as this the trees were still standing. Instead of the flattened growth seen in the English designs, I saw trees of a different shade of green, almost as though they had less chlorophyll in the leaves. There was a very large center circle and an outer ring closer than seen in the Celtic crosses. The four outer satellite circles were very small and precise.

The shade of green of these four circles was even lighter than the inner circle. I mentioned earlier visualizing four funnels running through the outer circles on designs in England. I see these also in the rain forest designs.

WITHIN & BEYOND: REVISITED

I perceive the message is one of hope, the planet is extremely adaptive but this does not give us the right to damage and destroy. With this message, I wondered what the other designs are telling the habitants of the planet.

There are some readers who may be querying this vision but it is not as strange it might first appear. There have been earth designs sited in the United States in fields of thistle. After scientific analysis of the circles, the experts discovered that there was new growth on the thistle plants, *completely different from the normal growth*. If a crop in the middle of a design can generate different leaves, is it not possible for giant trees in a rain forest to produce different leaves.

Arthropods

We know this category of life by the various common names, including ants, spiders, lobsters, crabs. As we look at earth designs of the world, we see many forms.

First: -- There are the crop circle designs, which include:

- July 17, 1997 East Meon Hampshire, an "***Ant***" (Lamb, p 90)

- June 1994, Barbury Castle, the "*Spider*", (Lamb, p 83)

- The next four appeared, from left to right, May, 1994, Silbury Hill. Bishops Cannings July, 1994. The last two appeared nearby shortly after these first two. "Scorpion, (Lamb, p81)

- *NASCA Spider* drawing

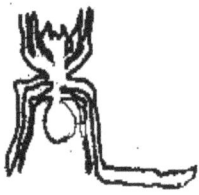

Second: -- We look to Peru to see the shape of a spider is in what is called the NAZCA lines. Experts think these lines were drawn in the desert around 200 BC; their origin continues to puzzle us.

Three: -- The previous two examples can be viewed or verified by the reader; this one cannot. While visiting the Yucatan, Mexico in September, 2002, Hurricane Isadora paid a visit.

As I sat on the shores of Campeche overlooking the Gulf of Mexico, I saw the hurricane in all its beauty. I am using the word "beauty" because at a distance it is just that. There is no visible destruction when you are sitting on a hotel deck overlooking the vast ocean. What I saw was an undulating ocean with turbulent clouds above, lit up by flashes of lightning. As these bursts brightened the sky an image of a large lobster or scorpion flashed on the water's surface.

Reviewing these three examples, I realized they covered more than 2,000 years in three different mediums – living crops, rock, and water. They included all elements of life.

Rock gives us the **earth**. Living crops require air to live and grow. In Mexico, **water** was the artist's canvass and the **fire** came from the lightning. Here we have an earth design that connects the elements, a mystery. Consequently, I decided to meditate on this mystery. This is what I was told.

We use spider, scorpion and ants as images because of their power. Many, many eons ago, this was the only life on your planet. Through their wisdom, they chose to create other life forms. However, these became weak and full of ego. The original forms have their own house, own food production and their own air. They are completely self-sufficient. As the other forms were created, each one was denied at least one requirement of life. This encouraged working with other life forms but it can lead to strife and desires. We use these images to remind all life form that when the greed of others becomes too strong, it is time to slow down or to back off. It is a reminder also that even though it may not appear so, each life form was created in such a way to be completely self-sufficient, provided the being does not crave what it does not have. Life as you see it is being prepared to do without what others have. All life in the universe has everything it needs and is complete unto itself.

Therefore, when these designs appear in a specific region, there is a need to step back and look at what is needed and what aspect is struggling.

Reflecting upon Mexico, I saw many reactions to the storm. Some people were distraught over material wealth and others were distraught over physical and human suffering. Perhaps the reader may research what occurred when the various designs manifested.

Rock Designs -- known & unknown sources

Here, the first two are mysteries which I discovered close to home. Since I found these so easily, I began wondering how many more you or I could find nearby without extensive searching.

Ape Caves:

This first one was an image from the Ape Caves in Washington State near Mt. St. Helens. The caves formed 2,000 years ago after a volcanic eruption. Today, it is just a long lava tube with ordinary gray granite rocks; at least how it appears to the naked eye. This was one of the few places where evidence of the eruption appeared. After the developed film came back to me, these rocks were deep orange color, not the original gray granite seen by the naked eye. This face appeared in five of the twenty-four pictures; no others shared this coloring.

WITHIN & BEYOND: REVISITED

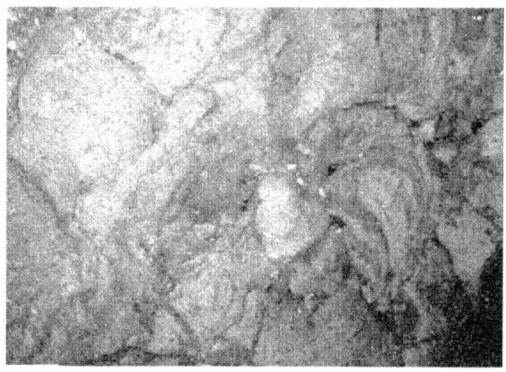

Shortly after this particular visit, I began channeling a new entity, an extremely old and loving energy. Now, he comes through regularly.

Every time I look at this face, I see a guardian and protector, not just of the cave itself but all the peoples. While I did not go deep into the tunnel of caves, I got a strong sense that it held many stories and secrets. This protection was not just of visitors but the entities that rest inside. I also got a sense that for complete protection, a person must be willing to accept the existence of these entities. The skeptic was not as well protected.

Another impression came when I sat near this rockface. I sensed a strong native presence. Consequently, I later researched the native history of the region. Unfortunately, I could not find any written information confirming or denying the existence of indigenous peoples in this specific region.

We do know, however, that humans migrated from Asia, across the Bering Straits and down through North America into South America. Logic then tells us that the Ancient ones must have stayed here for a period of time.

X Á:YTEM

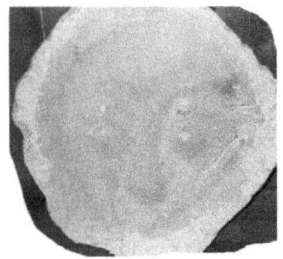 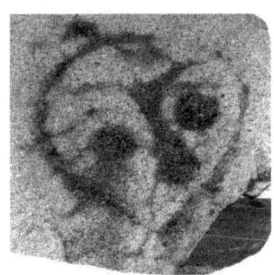

The second native rock design has two parts, each show a face embodied in stone. While they are known as petroglyphs, I am reluctant to use this term. Traditionally, a petroglyph is a *figure carved into a rock.* These images, particularly the first one, appear to be far deeper than what can be achieved by carving, even if we allow for time erosion to soften the edges. I will continue to use the term rock designs; the origin is unknown.

The **Stó:lō** First Nation is holding them in trust at their Native Interpretive Longhouse Center in Mission, British Columbia, Canada. This center is built upon an ancient village that is more than 9,000 years old, an appropriate resting place for the petroglyphs. The Katzic rocks designs (petroglyphs) were discovered on Chawathil First Nation land near Hope, 50 kilometers (30 miles) from Xá: ytem. Until such time as the Chawathil Nation has an appropriate display facility, the rock designs will stay with the **Stó:lō** First Nation at Xá: ytem.

Anxious to get more information, I called Dr. Linnea Battel, Director of X̱á:ytem. I learned that the faces are those of **X:als** the creator and transformer. Both the site of discovery and X̱á:ytem are sacred sites for the **Stó:lō** people.

Also at this Center is an enormous rock, called the transformer. Both the rock and the location are high energy and carry strong spiritual power. Although there were faces and images on the giant rock, they were more obscure and did not photograph well. However, as I pondered each of these, I picked up the same gentle energy shared by the other two faces. I also picked up a strong parental energy that challenged visitors to behave.

Looking at the faces that did photograph well, I find the first face extremely gentle and playful. As I viewed it, I had a strong desire to giggle with happiness. This emotion was carried through many years. The second image is more serious and much more of a guardian. Throughout my visit, I got a strong sense of love, caring and well-being.

Viewing all these faces, the Ape caves and Xá:ytem together, I sense a great age in all three; all holding enormous wisdom. The Ape Cave face comes across with grandfatherly love, the first Xá:ytem face that of an uncle and the third that of a parent. While all three faces carry love and protection, they disseminate it in different ways, just as it is in our daily lives.

Irish statue

This statue is not a normal earth design, as defined according to the definitions included here. I am including it though because of the similarity between the faces of the Xá: ytem rocks and the statues of Northern Ireland.

This particular head is from one of the more famous statues in Ireland, specifically Northern Ireland. Although you see the head image in many places, this particular one was found in a cemetery on Boa Island in Lower Lough, Erne County, Northern Ireland.

Described as a Janus statue because of the two heads back to back; it dates well before Christian times. The eyes are different shapes but the faces are the same shape with the same large nose. As I pondered each one separately, I got similar feelings or sensations.

- Romans describe Janus as custodian of the Universe and new beginnings.
- The Irish describe this as a God stone of fertility.
- The Stó:lō face is that of **X:als,** their creator -- is that not the custodian of the Universe?
- These three regions are thousands of miles apart and did not share ancestry for some time to come, yet have similar earth designs.
- Also, the time-line does not correlate.

The Xá:ytem faces are approximately 9,000 years old. Archaeologists date the Irish statue back approximately 2,000 years old to Celtic times.

However, based on other artifacts found, it would not be unnatural to assign the creation of this statue on their beliefs.

At this time, we have only speculation but there is enough information available to ponder the actual source of the design. Currently, though the answer is not available.

WITHIN & BEYOND: REVISITED

Historical Stones or Tablets of the World

Tablets are not always earth designs as they are defined, however the age, similarities and the information carved upon each one is pertinent.

The Egyptian Rosetta stone does not need an introduction, since it is already infamous. It was discovered in 1799 in the town of el-Rashid, hence the English name Rosetta. The other two tablets are also old and contain information yet to be deciphered. The writing or drawings are similar to that of the peoples of the area.

The Easter Island *Rongo-rongo Tablets* were discovered approximately 500 years ago. They differ from other discoveries that we are writing about as they are wooden, not stone. Later, explorers noted in their journals that every home had a wooden tablet but nobody could decipher the engravings. Oral teachings tell us that they were brought by the first colonist, Hotu Matua. Was this the same as the creator of other cultures?

This next tablet is stone, not wood. The *Okinawa Rosetta* stone was discovered off Okinawa Island in the Philippine waters of Japan. The images are not hieroglyphic as the previous two; rather they appear much more basic symbology.

There have been attempts at deciphering them but at the time of this writing, there is no consensus to meaning.

Okinawa Rosetta

The ICA Stones of Peru

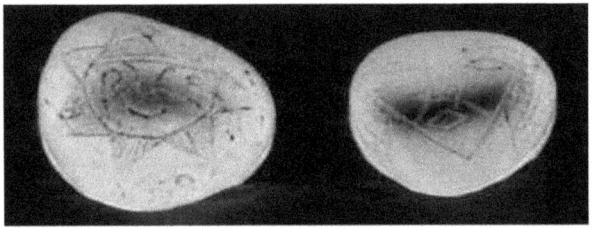

These designs must stand in a section by themselves. Hundreds of these stones were discovered in Peru, and kept hidden in a locked room at the Ica Stone Museum for some time by Dr. Javier Cabrera.

Barbara Hand Clow, in her book "*Catasrophobia: The Truth behind the Earth Changes*" estimates that they may be more than 175 million years old. Clow goes on to suggest that they "may be the library of a people at the peak of their evolution circa 15,000 to 10,500 B.C."

Some of the patterns illustrated on the Website look very similar to the NASCA lines. ICA is near the shores of Peru aligned with these lines. Should we now ask: Are the lines this old as well? Two stones that bore different markings are these two stones, known as *healing stones*. The following text is quoted from the Website of Robert Peters and Kathy Doore. At the time of writing this came from Doore's website – http://www.labrinthina.com

> *"The two stones seem to be a matched pair holding male- female polarities in a dynamic, harmonic balance. The "star" stone is more masculine. The "ET face" stone more feminine. Together, they seem to hold the full spectrum of frequencies - yin-yang, above-below, within-without. However, this is not a rigid absolute as they each also seem complete and whole. This is a positive note for male-female relationships, complete with communion.*
>
> *The "star" stone looks like a seven-pointed star with a human face, with possible connections to the Seven Sisters of the Pleiades.*
>
> *Dr. Cabrera writes of the Ica-Pleiades connection in his book. The Brotherhood of the Seven Rays (sometimes known as the "Great White Brotherhood" and/or Elohim) may have association with the enigma. The cross-hatch screen pattern on the forehead of the star (over the third eye) indicates clairvoyant abilities.*
>
> *The screen is literally a "screening device" which both concentrates and refines the incoming energy, so that only truth prevails. Looking*

> *at the star stone sideways, the "nose" can be seen as a male lingam penetrating the womb, which is shaped like a vesica piscis. The "mouth" is then the back of the cervix, and the eyes the testicles. Divine-human "intercourse" in all forms is empowered and facilitated by this stone including channeling and use of solar energy, star energy, kundalini and other energies of various kinds. The source is pure, versatile and inexhaustible.*
>
> *The "ET face" stone features large ears shaped like leaves, the cross-hatch pattern on these ears indicate clairaudient abilities with screening properties, which is borne out by personal experience. This stone has a flat surface on the face and fits perfectly on the forehead over the third eye. A continual stream of power, wisdom, love and bliss streams through this stone into the one working with it. Both stones are empathic, and highly relational. They are tuned in to the handler, giving him what is needed most while interacting with him as well."*

This piece of text parallels many of the points I tried to make in this book. It speaks of the star; I speak of a star tetrahedron. It speaks of harmonic balance; I speak of harmonic balance. Although the writing doesn't specifically call them signs, the carvings match some of my signs nevertheless.

While the collection does not label it as such, when I pondered the stone shown below, I got the feeling of a healing stone. For this reason, I named it the Ica Fern Tree.

WITHIN & BEYOND: REVISITED

There are some who will disagree, but I see this as a tree, a sacred tree carrying information and keys to spatial transportation.

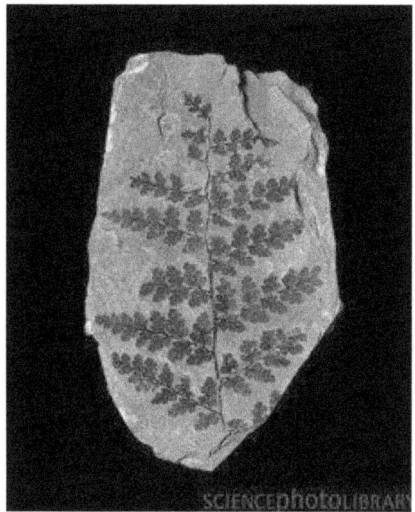

Ica Fern Tree

These are only a few of the many stones with mysterious designs or origins discovered around the globe. One thing they do have in common is the hosting of similar energy. I believe that this energy is gifted from other beings to humans and it is this energy that gives them the ability to carve the designs.

Not too long after seeing this image, I decided to take images of all three stones (two healing stones and the Ica stone) into a meditation. Before I began, I placed a picture of the healing stones on the table in front and the image of the tree into the palm of my hand. Immediately I was filled with energy and began seeing pictures of other planets and life styles.

Whenever I surveyed stones with mysterious designs or origins from around the globe, I sensed the one thing they had in common was parallel energy.

For two stones or rocks to carry similar energy they require a high content of crystal. For example, the ICA stones carved out of Andesite which is a gray to black volcanic rock. They are approximately 50% silica which matches quartz crystal. When the crystal content is high, there are two results.

First, humans receive the ability to carve the designs. During the time when the stones were placed upon the earth, the entire universe communicated telepathically. There is a telepathic communication either between humans or between a human and energies from beyond the earth plan that we get a particular trait activated. Regrettable, this ability diminished over time resulting in only a few being able to communicate this way. Fortunately, the trend is changing and we are seeing an increase in telepathy.

Secondly, the high crystal content assists in balancing our MANU NYMBA, helping us to connect with our Cosmic Life Pattern and therefore interpret the many signals or messages. Also, objects such as the healing stones generate their healing power when the holder, specifically the owner or giver of the healing, has their MANU NYMBA in balance.

Earth designs are discovered when someone is near the location whose MANU NYMBA is so completely balanced that messages can be sent, and heard, from beyond the earth plane. The fact that most people today have a balanced MANU NYMBA explains the increased number of findings. To use a cliché: the timing is right. When the ICA stones were unearthed by a flood, I also see this as more evidence of the right timing.

When I look at the Ica Fern Tree stone, I realize that sacred trees have been with us for millions of years and transcend our planet into their worlds. I may never know the meaning of this tree in this lifetime, but I see many possible interpretations. This stone is a gift for humanity.

The telepathic connection occurs with either with two or more humans or an earth human and energies beyond the Earth Plane when the MANU NYMBA is so completely balanced that messages can be sent, and heard, beyond the earth plane. Objects such as healing stones generate their healing energy when the holder has the MANU **NYMBA** in balance. This does not refer to the patient, if you want to label, but the owner of the stones or giver of the healing. The signs were received at such times as my MANU NYMBA was in balance and I was open to receive information. However, since I am a young novice compared to energies beyond, I was only given partial information.

When the healing stones were placed upon the Earth, the entire universe communicated telepathically. If you stepped out of your body and become a simple energy being in the universe, you would 'hear' or feel the information. It is like an inner knowing.

The sacred trees carry the information that allow this inner knowing to transfer it to a sentient being who is able to use the information appropriately.

The Ica Fern Tree stone reminds us that sacred trees have been with us for millions of years and transcends our planet into other worlds. The meaning of this tree will probably never be known in this lifetime. We do know however that they are gifts for humanity. Some uses have been utilized.

The aborigines of Australia are good examples of people who know how to pull their MANU NYMBA into balance, communicate and shape-shift and gain knowledge needed at a particular time.

It is important to understand that the communication through the MANU NYMBA is different than the MER-KA-BA, not better or worse, just different. It is the crystal clusters that are connected to the MANU NYMBA makng the communication possible, much like radios.

One key to understanding is the use of numbers. Many cultures used numbers, especially in their calendars. The Maya calendar is used by many. Elder Hunbatz Men of Mexico created one that can be applied to the ICA Fern. The following is what he interpreted:

1. There are three clusters of fronds and three circles in each side. In the Tzolk'n calendar, three represents the *trinity*. In the days of the month, three is *cimil* and means *finish, change, remove* or *disappear*. In the month, three is *zip* and means *ripeness, usefulness, completeness,* or *availability*.
2. There are five fronds on each side and another five at the top, for a total of fifteen. (Fifteen reduces to six). In the Tzolk'n calendar, five means *move about*. In the days of the month, five is *lamat* meaning *penetrate, examine, deepen,* or *analyze*. In the months, it means *ingenuity, curiosity, perseverance* or *quest*.
3. There is a total of six circles plus the six from the total fronds. In the Tzolk'n calendar, six means *sprout* or *hatch*. In the days of the month, six is *muluc*, meaning *near, around, adjacent,* or *close. In the months, it means goal, purpose, end* or *cycle*.

WITHIN & BEYOND: REVISITED

Looking at these interpretations, I see the Ica Fern Tree as a sacred tree helping people on their quest of completion and answers. The six circles bring senses of life and new beginnings. Perhaps more answers will come as they are frequently held.

Putting It All Together; Making It Work

So far you have received a great deal of food for thought. Some of it is information only; other pieces can be used to continue your personal growth. There are four ways to use this information.

1. Accept it or ponder, then store it in your personal memory bank.
2. Create drawings or collect pictures and hold them during a meditation.
3. Create temporary obelisks for sacred space and meditations.
4. Develop specific meditations where you call upon healing and balancing properties.

1. Accept it or ponder

Since this book includes new concepts and old information, you may want to reserve comment until you complete more research. This way of using the information is simply to put it on your bookshelf.

2. Create drawings or collect pictures

For effective collection of information, drawings do not have to be complex and sophisticated. If you find picture copies of your personal sacred tree, crystal skull, or earth design, you can place them inside a triangle, at the three points or hold them during your special healing sessions.

When I use the word triangle, you can replace it with the word pyramid if this is more comfortable for you. To make this change you make the triangle three dimensional with the center point sending the power down to the object in a central energy shaft.

Working with objects inside a triangle or MANU NYMBA shape, I find, requires a small triangle that can be placed either immediately in front of you during a seated session or upon an altar-like table. A triangle pulls the energy from the center to the sides.

What is on the corners or edges receives the benefit. This then flows out to the surrounding areas. Compare this to an earth energy vortex. Everything around the vortex receives the benefit.

Using the MANU NYMBA model is powerful. Placing the symbol or image of whatever you are using into the Supercharged Core spreads the energy through the entire star tetrahedron.

For example, if you are using a sacred tree, then a picture or piece of the tree would go into the core. Alternatively, a skull, picture of skull or a healing stone would go into the core. If you sit near this, you will find the energy will flow into your entire body, balancing the network.

There are two ways to work with images or objects on the corners instead of the middle. First, the structure must be large enough to allow you to sit inside. For a triangle, you would simply sit in the middle. For the MANU NYMBA, you would sit on the Supercharged Core. This is extremely healing and balancing. However, it requires a large space.

The principle behind a triangle also applies to a pyramid. If you are sitting in a pyramid, and you are accustomed to pulling or sending energy, then you align your crown chakra with the center point above you and proceed to move the energy.

3. Create temporary obelisks

This is a wonderful, playful technique. We all like to be creative regardless of our ability, and this is a way to achieve two goals. The first goal is creative and the second one is utilizing the information you are receiving.

An air-dry molding plaster is a suggestive method for creating one. This product is generally overnight drying and can be shaped, molded and drawn on for some time the next day. However, I recommend that you have a plan such as what images you are putting on it and what paints, if any, are you using.

For the most effective use of this type of meditative obelisk, I recommend using a malleable molding product. Pliable children's plasticine or a similar product works very well. The advantage of a product such as this is you can listen to your inner voices, or guides, and then draw the appropriate sign for a particular time.

This may be a sign to balance you. It may be a sign that brings in new, pertinent information. What is required for balancing depends on so many factors that it is almost impossible to have a solitary technique. As we evolve, we are continually opening to new information.

Another use for a malleable obelisk is to correct minor imbalances in the body. As you prepare the material, if your body is low in a particular vitamin, mineral or similar nutrient, you will be told. Then, you can take a pill or capsule and embed it into the obelisk. During the meditation where you are holding the structure in your hand, the necessary nutrients will be transferred to your hand and absorbed through the skin.

4. Develop specific meditations

Incorporating the pieces of information such as crystal skulls can be achieved with any method or procedure of meditation techniques. However, if you want to ensure your MANU NYMBA network is aligned, growing and working as it should, then you need to work with explicit methods.

Using these techniques will still make it possible to align your MANU NYMBA *and* get new information in one session, providing your body needs only minor alignment. To achieve complete balance, you can use several methods.

Aligning using sound and color

Previously we spoke of the strength and power of vibrational energy within our body. We know that the MANU NYMBA is this energy. Therefore, it is not surprising that the most effective way to balance the MANU NYMBA in our body would be to use the vibrational energy of sound and color. While this is the most effective way, unfortunately, it can also be the most expensive and the most structured. It requires equipment, a structured environment and the help of another person. In spite of these constraints, I recommend using this procedure whenever possible.

For a complete balance, you want to start at the base of the earth tetrahedron, using a low A and the color green, mov-

WITHIN & BEYOND: REVISITED

ing up through the two tetrahedrons and then taking a small step back to finish off balancing the Supercharged Core.

Your objective is to move through the tones smoothly and evenly at the same time as when your client visualizes the even wave of the spectrum of colors flowing from one point to the next. It is very important always to move up the scale. Moving in the opposite direction can throw a person into even greater imbalance.

Preparation

You will need:

1. A complete set of good quality tuning forks
2. A clear uncluttered corner of a room, or a large screen that arcs around the client's back to reverberate the sound. You want the tone to echo BACK from the screen or corner into all parts of the client's body.
3. A comfortable straight chair.
4. For the first few times, it may be necessary to have an information sheet with the procedural steps (below) written out.
5. Having this table of information copied from earlier text in front of both of you. This lets both of you see the flow of the tones and the colors.

Musical Note	Specific Tetrahedron -- **Magnet or** Electrical	Color
Low-G	Magnetic	Green
A	Magnetic	Yellow
B	Magnetic	Orange

C	Magnetic	Red
D	Electrical	Violet
E	Electrical	Indigo
F	Electrical	Blue
Hi-G	Electrical	Blue-Green
	Magnetic	White
	Electrical	Gold
		Blue & Red

Procedure, Part One

1. Have the person sit in the corner or in front of the screen, facing out with feet flat on the floor. You will stand approximately five feet in front of the person.
2. Line up all the tuning forks in an ordered row. – Low A > B > C > D > E > F > G > High A. These will take the tuning first through the magnetic tetrahedron moving evenly to the electrical tetrahedron.
3. Explain that as you are sounding each fork, the client should visualize the corresponding color for each note before switching over to the next color in the flow for the appropriate next note. This flow would be:
    a) Low A – Green
    b) B: yellow
    c) C: Red
    d) D Blue
    e) E: Orange
    f) F: Purple
    g) G: Indigo
    h) High A: Green

WITHIN & BEYOND: REVISITED

4. Subjects should close their eyes and "see" the wave of the color flowing from the first color to the second throughout the entire run.
5. Until the person is completely familiar with the tones and colors, as you move through the tuning forks, inform the person which particular color to visualize.
6. As you move from one fork to the next, allow the previous fork to continue vibrating.
7. When you finish sounding the High A fork, allow it to become completely still.
8. Sweep the client's energy field from head to toe and allow the person to remain calm for a couple of minutes before moving onto the next procedure.

Procedure, Part Two

One of the purposes of Part One is to clear each separate part of the MANU NYMBA. Part Two aligns the MANU NYMBA into a specific pattern, which moves the energy from one point to the next It is a means to strengthen the Supercharged Core.

This order was explained as follows: Make the following changes to the procedures in Part One.

1. Line the tuning forks up in the following order: **C, >G, >B, >E, >Low A, >F, >D, > High A**
2. Explain that as you sound each fork, the person should visualize each note with the corresponding color switching over to the next color in the flow for the appropriate note. After several sessions, the flow will develop a definite rhythm. This flow would be:
    a) C: Red
    b) G: Indigo

c) B: Yellow
   d) E: Orange
   e) Low A: Green
   f) F: Purple
   g) D: Blue
   h) High A: Green
3. As before, allow the tuning forks to stop completely at the end and then sweep the person's energy field from head to toe. Let the clients return to the present in their own time.

Meditations

There are numerous techniques that are effective; these three mediation techniques are favorites. The first two are for personal healing or seeking information. The first is silent, the second uses a mantra. The third healing method sends healing to a person or persons. Either of the first two will work with a triangle or pyramid when you bring in an object as described in the first part of this section.

Method One – Silent meditation

Step One: Going into the Meditation.

If you do not have a favorite method or are unfamiliar with meditation then I recommend the following:

1. To help you focus, have soft, gentle music playing quietly in the background.

2. Sit upright in a comfortable chair with your hands in your lap, palms facing up, and your feet solid on the ground, parallel to each other.
3. Breathing slowly, taking three deep breaths. Breathe in to the count of four, hold for four, and slowly breathe out to a count of four. Repeat this three times.
4. On the third intake, hold your breath, ask for healing for yourself or others (giving names) or move to Step II.

Step II: Asking questions

When you ask questions in a meditation, be careful not to ask too many and ensure the ones you do ask are all on the same topic. If you ask too many questions, you end up not getting any answers. I frequently see the spirit guides throwing their imaginary hands up in the air. This is one occasion where it is appropriate to do a little planning. Some suggestions are:

- What characteristics do I need at this time to improve the balance of my MANU NYMBA and my crystal cluster?
- If it is appropriate, please tell me what planet I need to connect with at this time.
- Please tell me the color and / or musical note that I need at this time.

If you are using sacred trees, signs, skulls, or earth designs in your meditation, it is quite appropriate to direct the questions around this tool. NOTE: If you do not get answers in a normal manner, then repeat what first comes into your mind. This is usually what is needed.

Method Two– Using a Mantra First
Purpose: Personal Balancing

Sit in the appropriate position for meditation. Take three breaths, using a count of four as outlined in Method one.

1. On the third breath intake, ask for guidance in balancing your internal MANU NYMBA.
2. To bring balance into your body, slowly repeat the mantra "MANU NYMBA". using a single syllable on each breathe either going out or coming into your body: -->MA -->NU -->NYM -->BA.
3. Continue repeating this mantra as long as necessary. After a while, you will be so deep into meditation that you are no longer aware of the words. Do not be concerned about whether you are doing it "right". Your body knows.

NOTE: If you are tuned into your body, you will feel a general alignment happening in your body. It is a great feeling.

Second Purpose: Healing Other Life Energies.

1. Sit in the appropriate position for meditation. Take three breaths, using a count of four as outlined above.
2. On the third breath intake, ask for guidance in balancing the MANU NYMBA belonging to another person or living entity. (Remember that societies are also living entities!).
3. As you are repeating the mantra, if the name of the entity is short enough to use all eight counts (four in, four out), then use it. For example if you have a

friend named Sally Rodgers who needs healing, then use as the whole mantra "SAL->LY->ROD->GERS->MA–>NU->NYM->BA". Otherwise, simply state who this mantra will be for and give the name. This is applicable for places with long names such as the United States. Regardless, use a single syllable on each breath either going out or coming into your body.
4. Continue repeating this mantra as long as necessary.

Energy Conduits

Previously, many methods of balancing and clearing the meridians or links in the body were introduced. Generally, the acupressure or acupuncture points are used. Science has proven that these points possess electrical conductivity. These points, then work extremely well for clearing and balancing the electrical tetrahedron.

Following this logic, we would have to assume that balancing the electrical tetrahedron would, simply through association, balance the magnetic tetrahedron. This assumption, though, is not always correct. For instance, if the crystal cluster is responsible for the imbalance, then you need to balance the magnetic tetrahedron directly. It is also possible that you muscle-checked the person and verified the need for magnetic tetrahedron alignment. For whatever reason, you may want a simple, direct, solution, solution that works for balancing the entire MANU NYMBA network.

Earlier, we demonstrated the linking of the MANU NYMBA complex network of conduits. What we stress is that *all* the conduits are connected to two main channels in the body running parallel to the meridians. This applies to wherever a network resides, in the human body, societies, tribes, or living entities in nature. Since they are so closer to the meridians, we can apply similar balancing techniques; just the name and intent will differ. These two conduits are the frontal and posterior conduits. For comparison, the two meridians are called the central and governing meridians.

Regardless of where the MANU NYMBA channels run, they carry both magnetic and electrical energy since they are made up of many MANU NYMBA. The frontal conduit runs up the front from the pubic area to the lower lip. The posterior conduit runs up the back from the base of the spine up and over the head to the upper lip.

When the energy is blocked in either of these channels, it affects the entire system. The energy blocks both electrical and magnetic pathways, taking the energy in and away from the earth and the sky.

There are two ways of unblocking these channels. Both use the energy of our bodies or an universal energy system known as Reiki energy.

1. The first way involves pressure points on the body. Explanations are found either in an acupuncturist's manual or in the *Touch for Health* manual. This system uses what it calls neuro-lymphatic and neuro-vascular points. Hold this position until you can feel a pulse at each end. Once you feel the pulse, shift your fingers slightly off center to pick up the appropriate conduit.
2. This way is often simpler. Hold your hand about one inch (3cm) away from the body. Starting at the base of the invisible channel, slowly run your hand from the base up the full length of the channel. Remove your hand completely from the body and repeat several

times. The reason we take the hand away completed is to prevent producing a counter effect. Moving the hand in the opposite direction negates the clearing we have just completed.

Since it is difficult to run your hand up your back and over your head in one uninterrupted flow, if the posterior conduit is blocked, solicit help from someone who is knowledgeable of the process.

Conclusion

This book introduces many concepts and small fragments of relevant information. Those who are able to feel the energy of the crop circles or any other design will undoubtedly have their MANU NYMBA in balance without even knowing. They will also be able to link the small fragments together. To achieve this, it is probable their body's crystal content is higher than normal and higher than that of their parents. If it was measurable, I am sure we would discover that the percentage of crystal content of the human being 2000 years ago was greatly smaller than it is today.

When a person with the high crystal content reads this book, they would think: *This makes sense*. Whether the crystal content is on the rise or not, humanity is at the point of receiving more information from other beings, the past and other worlds. We are awakening and ready to receive universal knowledge including what the Pleiades through Lemuria people, stored on the earth so long ago.

If these data seem strange and you want clarification, then the techniques at the end of the book will help bring you into balance. Remember:

> *Where energy follows thought, thought directs energy and change follows.*

Throughout the messages and information I have received over the past twenty years, the recurring theme was balance. Sometimes, it has even been annoyingly repetitive! Ancient health systems such as Ayurveda and TCM recognize balance as a key to good health and long life. Understanding the MANU NYMBA is just one more path to this balance.

Balance and CLP access does not need to be melodramatic. This book includes resources that have been around for thousands of years. Some were used only in rituals, perhaps only by shamans. Others were available to entire populations. As we travel through time and visit ancient cultures, we discover the importance of *inner knowing*. In most societies, inner knowing came from balance and the ability to interpret signs and messages from the CLP. When you "hear" or feel information, then you must have inner knowing.

It is important to reiterate that the communication through the MANU NYMBA differs from communication through the MER-KA- BA. It's not better or worse, just different. The intent is quite different. Using crystals when working with the MANU NYMBA enhances the CLP contact.

While you can use crystals when you work with the MER-KA-BA, to my knowledge there are no specific exercises in the MER-KA-BA program.

As we continued to evolve and the crystal arms of the MANU NYMBA have grown, it helped balance us. In addition, it opens up ability so that we see things we couldn't see before, such as crop circles and designs in stones. This is what is happening with the crystal skulls. It isn't just the energy passing between the skulls but the link with messages left in the temples.

Albert Einstein once said:

> *The most beautiful experience we can have is the mysterious. It is the fundamental emotion which stands at the cradle of true art and science. Whoever does not know it and can no longer marvel is as good as dead, and his eyes are dimmed.*

I hope many of you will explore the mystery and discover the many alternative ways to communicate and receive information. Writing this book has been a challenge, but it has also been illumination with the new information and truths sent to me by my spirit friends.

To close, I quote an ancient friend of all of us who said:

What is a friend? A single soul with two bodies Aristotle, 384-322 BCE.

Biography

This is a revision of Gayle Redfern's third publication. All of her writings have come out in 2nd editions.

Gayle is a conscious channel and psychic. Her recent career has included work as a health practitioner, psychic work and spiritual guidance.

Although she still does readings for clients, her focus today is writing. Her first book, *Inner Bridges,* was completely channeled, emphasizing inner health and inner balance. Her second book, *Ayurveda Demystified* drew on her holistic health knowledge by simplifying the language of Ayurveda and introducing it to the Western world.

This book *Within & Beyond revisited*, is the 2nd edition of her third book *Within & Beyond.* Both of these books are spirit guided, and show us what we can gain when we have inner balance and peace. Here, her spirit friends introduce you to completely new information and trust that it has been explained it in such a way that people could understand and apply it to their lives.

Once upon a time is **NOW...**
 ...a New Age exploration
Into the meaning of existence.

The past is coming and the future has passed. Everything in this book is true, and it's exactly how it has always been and always will be. This sentence became the cornerstone of this writing. I was continually given images and information that was new and strange. I knew it was old knowledge,

...and it all made sense!

You and I have the challenge of interpreting the facts and expanding our horizons. Throughout history we have been given many gifts, and now we are being shown how to access them---PLUS blend them into our lives.

The Cosmic Life Pattern is an integral part of our being. It opens the doors to the wonders of the crystal skulls, crop circles and other mysterious phenomena. I invite you to explore this thought provoking information.

Wisdom begins in wonder...

...Socrates

Editorial Review from Amazon.com

Product Description

It is time for humanity to look at the topic of "dimension" and "time "differently. This book, *Within and Beyond* by **Gayle Redfern** looks at these and other pertinent issues. What is rapidly becoming apparent is the fact that everyone has simultaneous access to ALL nine planes of reference and has had this access since before birth. Using our Planes of Reference, as I define dimensions, we can view or interpret any piece of information 9 different ways. The planes are nothing other than placing our attention on a portion of our reality or what is seen.

This book is not about physical attributes of the human. Regardless, just as the genetic coding protected some people in the Middle Ages, today the Cosmic Life Pattern (CLP) protects some people from various ailments and opens up specific sources of more information. Therefore, as you move through this book, you need to remember that not everyone gets messages from rocks or sacred trees, crystal skulls or crop circles. We will all receive information; the source just won't be the same as your neighbours.

Like so many other books, this book was not written in order from beginning to the end. Instead it started with data fitting into the middle of the book. For more than two years there was no pattern to the incoming information, it jumped from section to section in no apparent order. For most of this time this simply confused and puzzled me. But when I realized this was nothing more than an example of no such thing as time I was able to set my confusion aside and let the information flow, knowing order would evolve. It was a reminder that order of any kind implies past, present and future time; one of three precepts in this book. As you move through the book, you will see these concepts intertwined. They are: 1) Planes of Reference, 2) Time versus no-time 3) Pleiadian energy.

I feel confident that when a person with the high crystal content reads this book they would think "This makes sense." Whether the crystal content is on the rise or not, humanity is at the point of receiving more information from other beings, the past and other worlds. We are awakening and ready to receive universal knowledge including what the Pleiadians, through Lemuria stored on earth so long ago.

If this data seems strange and you want clarification, then the techniques at the end of the book will help bring you into balance. Remember: - Where energy follows thought, thought directs energy and change follows.

Milton Keynes UK
Ingram Content Group UK Ltd.
UKHW010500050324
438776UK00005BB/674